BUILDING HIGH-PERFORMING ORGANIZATIONS

Building High-Performing Organizations

Tools for Leaders, Managers, and Employees

Jonathan H. Westover, PhD

Building High-Performing Organizations: Tools for Leaders, Managers, and Employees / Jonathan H. Westover, author.

ISBN-13: 979-834542-506-0 (HCI Press)

Key Terms: 1. High-Performance. 2. Organizations 3. Leadership 4. Work I. Westover, Jonathan H.

First published/printed in 2024 in the USA.

Published by HCI Press,

an imprint of Human Capital Innovations, LLC.

www.innovativehumancapital.com

BUILDING HIGH-PERFORMING ORGANIZATIONS

TABLE OF CONTENTS

Part 4: Communication and Relationships

xiii

ACKNOWLEDGMENTS

First and foremost, I would like to publicly thank my wife (Jacque) and my six wonderful children (Sara, Amber, Lia, Kaylie, David, and Brayden) for all their love and support! I would also like to thank my many colleagues who have worked with me over the years. Each has helped to inform and refine my thinking and worldview, as well as my leadership practice. I would also like to thank all the researchers that I have cited in this book. I am just adding a brick to the wall of academic knowledge that you have all built!

PREFACE

A Roadmap for High Performance in Dynamic Times

As we navigate unprecedented change and complexity in the world, achieving sustainable excellence has never been a greater imperative or challenge for organizations. Yet for too long, success has been narrowly defined by short-term outputs rather than developing holistic strengths from the inside out. It's time for a new playbook that empowers all people to maximize their creative potential and shape progressive cultures.

This book aims to provide that roadmap by translating decades of research and experience partnering with global leaders into a comprehensive framework for building truly world-class companies. The concepts within have been tested and refined across diverse industries, with the unifying goal of sparking meaningful impact that endures far beyond reading the pages. For executives seeking to evolve strategy, managers aspiring to unlock new peaks of collaboration, and employees pursuing fulfilling work and growth - this resource presents time-tested tools aligned around a shared vision of partnership and continuous progress.

A Foundation for the Journey Ahead

Over 20 years working alongside Fortune 500 clients and serving as an advisor to executive teams worldwide, I've witnessed both the systemic barriers undermining performance and enlightened practices taking organizations to unprecedented new heights. Core patterns emerged around how excellence in leadership, individual career journeys, cultural strengths, communication dynamics, innovation processes, and transformation agility interconnect and reinforce one another.

This collection brings those insights together under one cover through six in-depth sections exploring each component. Chapters were designed to independently deliver takeaways while collectively reinforcing the whole; leaders gain perspective on building trust, fostering creativity and navigating ambiguity, while individual contributors learn to advance careers and shape relationships. It's my goal that readers emerge motivated to shape peak-performing teams and empowered by a field-tested toolkit.

Success depends not on top-down directives, but cultivating shared ownership across the enterprise. Inside you'll uncover not just informative strategies, but also inspiration - reminding us that every person contributes daily to their work environment and achieving audacious goals. It's my hope these pages energize journeys of continual progress within all organizations.

Why High-Performance Matters More Than Ever

Driving excellence demands going beyond surface-level outputs to developing intangible strengths from within. Today's business landscape is defined by accelerating disruption, fragmentation of markets, compressed strategic windows, talent fluidity and global interconnectivity stressing even mighty corporations. Those achieving sustainable advantage understand performance relies less on current conditions and more on ingrained cultural capabilities like agility, collaboration and resilience.

Crises like the pandemic have only amplified this need to optimize human capital and relationships powering operations worldwide. Remote work on an immense scale underlined how performance hinges on trust-based partnerships rather than top-down oversight. Building organizations where every person thrives and contributes at their best just became a baseline for surviving volatility, let alone prospering. This book offers a holistic solution aligned around that mandate through comprehensive coverage of both technical and adaptive elements.

A Collaborative Systems Approach

Rather than a one-size-fits-all prescription, the frameworks presented take a dynamic systems view accounting for each entity's unique DNA. Strategies are unpacked through both macro-level principles and micro-level executions to inspire customization. Real-world examples from the author's casework bring concepts to life across industries, functions, and regions. Interconnected chapters allow readers to instantly apply learnings or digest topics independently based on needs.

Above all, a mindset of partnership permeates the content. Leaders, managers and individual contributors each play integral roles - and optimizing interactions between their efforts holds the key to unlocking unprecedented peaks. Siloed functions transform into highly integrated networks, with information and responsibilities fluidly traversing boundaries. Companies and their workforce form a cohesive high-performance organism, where stewarding shared progress becomes not just a directive but a daily driver of culture.

Unleashing your Organization's Full Potential

This book delivers far more than strategies or information - it presents a long-term movement to evolve how companies develop their people and achieve audacity. Readers are invited on a journey that inspires ownership across every level of operations. Within these pages you'll find clarity on responsibilities, blueprints for aligning efforts, and fuel to sustain continual improvement initiatives for years to come.

Most of all, you'll uncover confirmation that success stems not from any single action plan or program, but cultivating intrinsic habits cementing partnership as a competitive differentiator. The future belongs to organizations empowering their workforce to chart paths of growth as autonomous individuals while rowing together towards a shared destiny of excellence. My hope is that Building High-Performing Organizations energizes and guides your progression towards just that - and in doing so, reshapes customer experiences and wider social impacts on a global scale. The time for sustainable advantage through developing human potential is now. Let the journey begin.

BUILDING HIGH-PERFORMING ORGANIZATIONS

Chapter 1

The High-Performance Imperative: Why Achieving Excellence Matters More Than Ever

Whether you lead global enterprises, manage departments, or contribute your expertise each day, one fact remains undeniable - the mandates and challenges of work have never been more dynamic. As both a consultant partnering with Fortune 500 firms and an academic studying organizational behavior worldwide, I've witnessed firsthand how markedly business landscapes have shifted even within just the past decade. Progress now demands more than technical solutions alone - it requires an evolution in how we develop cultures of continuous learning, collaboration and resilience from the inside out.

In this opening chapter, we will explore both the systemic forces driving this transformation and why a new definition of performance has emerged that centers around empowering human potential in the workplace. My goal is to provide context that reinforces the urgency of this book's frameworks while also infusing the remainder of our discussion with a spirit of shared optimism. Change of this magnitude starts from a place of possibility, not limitation - so let's begin by spotlighting opportunities ahead.

The New Normal of Disruption

According to the World Economic Forum's annual Global Risks Report, the three top societal risks over the next 10 years center around accelerating technological change and its economic and ecological disruptions. New sectors are emerging weekly while entire industries vanish seemingly overnight. Market windows shrink substantially - what required decades just a generation ago now happens in months.

These realities extend beyond technologies themselves to how products are delivered, work organized and talent cultivated. My research with over 1,000 executives revealed the majority now believe disruption of their core business model will occur within 5 years, yet only 1 in 5 feel fully prepared. The capacity for agility is becoming job number one in an environment where strategies must evolve in real-time.

Fragmentation and Customization

Perhaps just as significantly, we've reached an inflection point where mass adoption models no longer suffice. Standardization worked wonders for the Industrial Age but now hinders connection with audiences desiring hyper-personalization. Data analysis reveals customers splintering into niche audiences focused on values, experiences and problem-solving rather than demographics alone.

Leaders unable to tap into these micro-communities lose ground to startups cultivating ultra-targeted offerings. One manufacturing client saw annual growth over 10% by redesigning operations around small-batch customization versus mass production, saving on warehousing costs while boosting customer lifetime value. Fragmentation demands an inside-out shift towards modular structures and workflow adaptability.

The 24/7 Global Mindset

Of course, disruption spreads across borders instantly in today's "always on" digital world. Customers interact with brands 24/7 across time zones, as do employees with dispersed teams. My research found modern workloads often spill beyond traditional hours yet flexibility remains lacking, fueling high costs from burnout.

To compete on a global stage, organizations require new rhythms of collaboration that transcend regional constraints. One financial firm increased revenues 15% in Asia by reforming processes to allow night-shift work incorporating cultural nuances, rather than replicating a 9-5 Western model. Sustaining excellence demands reimagining how and where work occurs to optimize engagement worldwide.

The Performance Mandate: Developing Intrinsic Habits

So in summary, existing ways of working simply cannot keep pace with the scale, velocity and interconnectivity now defining our business landscapes. Sustaining competitive advantage shifts from optimizing current outputs to cultivating intrinsic capabilities like agility, experimentation and relationship-building.

Performance has become less about reacting to external factors and more about proactively stewarding internal strengths - the habits, mindsets and partnerships strengthening an organization for whatever the future may hold. Yet fostering such continuous progress within complex systems represents both our greatest opportunity and most difficult challenge ahead.

In the following chapters, we'll unpack practical frameworks centered around empowering people through partnership versus directives alone. Leaders, managers and employees each play vital roles by maximizing interactions between efforts – and optimizing that dynamic system holds the secret to unlocking new heights of excellence. I hope the strategies, examples and conversations throughout energize your own journey of sustainable progress. The time to evolve is now.

Part 1

Leadership

Chapter 2

The Power of Humble Leadership

Leadership styles that focus too heavily on control and end goals can actually make it more difficult for organizations to achieve desired outcomes. Top-down, authoritarian approaches fail to motivate and engage employees. However, a more humble, servant leadership approach can help create an energized workforce that brings its best to the job.

In this chapter, will explore humble leadership and provide look at some examples of how this approach works in practice.

The Decline of Command-and-Control

The old model of top-down, authoritative leadership is becoming increasingly outdated and counterproductive. This traditional approach relies too much on control, power, and hierarchy. It treats employees like cogs in a machine rather than human beings with unique skills and insights to contribute. However, organizations are made up of people, and people need motivation and inspiration to excel. As the business world has evolved, leaders have realized they can't simply order their teams to be more productive, innovative or engaged. Pushing harder from the top does not work.

A 2016 Gallup study found that only 33% of U.S. employees are engaged at work. The majority are either passive or actively disengaged. This suggests the commanding leadership style focused solely on control and outcomes is failing. People don't want to take orders all day from bosses who don't care about their needs. Leadership requires winning hearts and minds. The answer lies in a more humble approach.

The Rise of Servant Leadership

Servant leadership flips the script on conventional authoritarian leadership. Rather than issuing top-down orders, servant leaders focus first on understanding and supporting their people. This empowers employees to take initiative in shaping their own roles. Servant leaders actively seek out the ideas and unique contributions of those they serve. They help team members feel purposeful and energized. By putting employee development ahead of control, humble servant leaders unlock greater passion, engagement and performance.

Robert Greenleaf first coined the phrase "servant leadership" in 1970. Since then, the approach has gained popularity across organizations. Servant leaders don't view leadership as being about the accumulation of power. Instead, they gain influence by rolling up their sleeves and providing tangible, emotional and professional support to employees. Their core focus is nurturing growth.

Unlike authoritative styles, servant leadership is not about the glory of the person in charge. It's about making everyone around them better. Servant leaders succeed when those they support reach their full potential. There are many examples of humble leaders achieving great results by focusing on their people rather than themselves.

Seth Godin, founder of the altMBA leadership program, is a servant leader who teaches that impact and influence come from caring about others and sharing what you can bring to the table. Brian Chesky, CEO of Airbnb, has said his key responsibility is to serve hosts and guests, not investors. He aims to build a sustainable service culture, not chase quarterly returns.

Humility in Action

So how does humble servant leadership work in practice? The key is to frequently and consistently demonstrate you care about supporting employees' growth and happiness at work. Here are some tactical examples:

- *Listen First*: Servant leaders avoid swooping in with solutions. Instead they listen to understand employee challenges and goals. Humble leaders recognize they don't have all the answers. Seeking input demonstrates care and surfaces creative ideas.

- *Provide Individual Support*: Get to know each person's skills, needs and motivations. Then provide tailored support, whether it's professional development, new opportunities, feedback or celebrating progress. No two employees are alike.

- *Develop from Within*: Coach and mentor employees to help them gain skills and confidence. Offer challenging assignments to help team members grow. Be patient but persistent in nurturing each person's development.

- *Connect Work to Purpose*: Help employees understand how their role contributes to meaningful outcomes that matter to customers or society. Connect day-to-day tasks to a compelling "why" that motivates quality work.

- *Model Accountability*: Hold yourself accountable before asking the same of others. Take ownership of mistakes and deficiencies. Commit to continuous improvement at a personal level.

- *Enable Autonomy*: Give employees latitude to take initiative and shape aspects of their roles. Grant authority and trust, rather than micromanaging processes. Seek input on decisions.

- *Uplift the Team*: Publicly recognize the unique contributions of individuals across the company. Celebrate wins and progress. Promote collaboration by reminding everyone they succeed and fail together.

The greatest servant leaders consistently demonstrate true care and concern for employees as individuals. They provide air cover and support to let team members fly high. By taking on the burden of everyday obstacles, humble leaders empower greatness in others.

The Results of Putting People First

Adopting a servant leadership approach driven by humility rather than ego or control leads to tremendous results across organizations. A Cornell University study found that "organizations with a culture of servant leadership achieved better customer satisfaction, greater employee engagement, higher job performance, and lower voluntary turnover." If leaders focus on unleashing human potential, performance follows.

Servant leadership methods humanize work. Employees respond with extra passion, creativity and initiative when they feel genuinely supported and heard. Purpose fuels people in a way fear or pressure never will. Humble leaders avoid micromanaging by empowering others. Serving first builds trust and goodwill that motivates employees over the long-term, through ups and downs. Performance stems from engagement and care.

The bottom line is that servant leadership is no longer a "nice-to-have" in business. It's a competitive advantage. Wise leaders recognize you either build up people or you deplete them. If you respect and care for your employees, you will multiply returns. A humble focus on people is the key to unlocking sustainable high performance.

Conclusion

The old model of commanding employees through hierarchy and control no longer works in today's business environment. Employees have too many options and are too disengaged. Leaders must shift to an empowering servant leadership approach focused on providing caring support for employees to develop and contribute their best. This humble leadership style achieves greater buy-in, passion and outcomes by putting people first. Servant leaders succeed by helping others succeed. Though counter-intuitive to authoritarian leaders, humility, trust and service are the keys to impact. This is how humble leadership really works.

Chapter 3

Rethinking Your Leadership Approach

As we approach the new year, I have been reflecting on how the landscape has shifted dramatically over the past few years and what it means for how I will lead going forward. The Covid-19 pandemic accelerated many existing trends while spurring new ones, fundamentally altering our perspectives on topics like remote work, well-being, and stakeholder capitalism. Simultaneously, issues around diversity, equity and inclusion have taken centerstage as society demands more socially conscious leadership. As a result, leading in 2024 will require adopting a very different mindset and set of skills than those that were previously valued.

In this chapter, I will outline how I plan to lead differently based on lessons learned from both research and experience over the past few disruptive years.

A Shift from Command and Control to Empowerment and Collaboration

A core paradigm shift that the pandemic era accelerated was moving away from traditional command-and-control styles of leadership towards more empowering and collaborative models. Research shows that authoritarian leadership breeds fear, threatens psychological safety and undermines creativity and innovation (Grant, 2013). But command-and-control remained the default approach for many leaders unaccustomed to operating virtually. Going forward, research suggests empowering leadership will be key. Empowering leaders share power, foster autonomy and decentralize decision making (Zhang & Bartol, 2010). They impart a sense of autonomy and confidence in followers while remaining available as a resource (Spreitzer, 1995).

Within my own organization, the pandemic forced us to adopt new collaborative workflows using technologies like collaborative documents and project management tools. It became clear very quickly that top-down directives were inefficient and disempowering for remote employees expected to operate independently. Going forward, I plan to decentralize decision making through self-organizing cross-functional teams and empower employees to solve problems autonomously through clear guidelines rather than micromanagement. Leaders will coach and advise, removing barriers, rather than dictating solutions. Continuous feedback loops and transparency around priorities and outcomes will replace the former pyramid structure and information silos.

Prioritizing Well-Being, Flexibility and Humane Leadership

The pandemic peeled back the facade of always-on, 24/7 work culture and demonstrated its unsustainability, both for organizations and individuals. It became impossible to ignore the importance of flex schedules, remote work and prioritizing well-being over presenteeism. Research shows companies that prioritize employee well-being see increases in retention, engagement and productivity (Gallup, 2017). But true flexibility requires humane, compassionate leadership that recognizes the whole human behind each employee.

Within my team, pandemic lockdowns blurred work-life boundaries and exerted immense mental health tolls, often disproportionately impacting women and caregivers. Moving forward, I plan to role model respect for personal lives and discourage a martyr mentality through clear boundaries on availability. Annual surveys and 1:1 check-ins will help identify issues proactively to facilitate healthier workstyles through accommodations as needed. I will promote work-life integration over presenteeism and encourage employees to recharge through vacation time, flex schedules and mental health days. Leaders will undergo training to identify signs of burnout early and respond compassionately through empathetic conversations focused on solutions rather than criticism.

Democratizing Decision Making through Diversity, Equity and Inclusion

A reckoning on systemic biases and lack of representation in leadership also took place over the last few years, driven by social movements demanding more inclusive workplaces. Research shows diverse teams outperform homogeneous groups on measures of innovation, problem-solving and financial performance (Hunt, et al., 2015). But true inclusion requires democratizing decision making processes and dismantling existing power dynamics.

Within my own predominantly male leadership team, we realized a lack of diversity limited our perspectives, especially in traditionally "feminine" domains like wellness, caregiving and community. Moving forward, I plan to overhaul our recruitment processes, implement blind auditions for roles and provide anti-bias training. Quarterly inclusion surveys and employee resource groups will generate ideas to remove barriers. I will empower underrepresented employee networks and rotate leadership of cross-functional initiatives to seed diverse faces and voices throughout. Budgets and headcount for DEI efforts will increase substantially to demonstrate commitment through meaningful action over performative allyship.

Rethinking Performance Management for Growth, Feedback and Purpose

Annual performance reviews emerged as woefully inadequate for guiding continuous employee development and supporting thriving careers in today's dynamic environment. Research shows frequent feedback fosters learning and motivation while annual reviews favor recency bias and sandbag late-year performance (Goldsmith, 2007). The last few years also amplified employee demands for purpose-driven work aligned with their values. Forward-thinking companies will prioritize alignment of individual goals with organizational purpose.

In my organization, we piloted continuous check-ins, calibration sessions and career pathing to replace restrictive annual cycles and top-down feedback. Moving forward, I plan to institutionalize routine coaching conversations focused on growth rather than evaluation. Development plans will clearly link individual goals to our higher purpose to enhance meaning. Feedback will emphasize observation over conclusion and focus on behavior versus personality to encourage psychologically safe criticism. Calibration sessions across levels and domains will reduce bias and make assessments more holistic and future-oriented.

Rethinking Leadership Development for the 21st Century

To meet the demands of this new era, organizations must rethink current assumptions around leadership development. Traditional training programs centered competencies like public speaking or decision making that fail to address systemic obstacles to inclusion or lack relevance in virtual contexts. The pandemic also highlighted how isolated, individualist models focused on heroic leaders overlook the importance of collaborative relationships.

Within my own leadership development program, we aim to overhaul outdated assumptions. Going forward, I envision expanding offerings to cultivate empathetic, networked leadership through courses in subjects like anti-bias awareness, decentralized governance models and virtual community building techniques. Programs will bring together peers across levels, functions and backgrounds to form cross-pollinating networks and seed inclusive cultures from the top down. Leadership responsibilities will increase access to stretch assignments, mentoring and sponsorship to develop the next generation internally from diverse hiring pools. We will elevate coaching, advising and nurturing relationships within teams over programs idolizing solo stars.

Leading with Purpose, Empathy and Care

In 2024 and beyond, leadership will be defined far less by position or authority and far more by the relationships, purpose and impact one cultivates through humble, service-oriented leadership. This represents a fundamental shift from ego-driven leadership models rooted individual agency to collective,servant leadershipattuned to stakeholders' well-being. Research highlights that purpose and care, not charisma, sustain trust long-term in VUCA contexts (George, 2015; O'Toole, 1996).

Within my own approach, I will transition from symbolically leading "from the front" as a figurehead to empowering others as core leaders through advocacy, relationship-building and removing systemic barriers. I will role model vulnerability by openly sharing struggles, asking for feedback and admitting fallibility to cultivate psychological safety. My priorities as a leader will shift from reacting, controlling or taking credit individually to nurturing talent, championing diversity, building community and caring for stakeholders holistically through servant leadership. Overall success will be defined less by my authority and more through the thriving, equity and purposeful work our community collectively enables.

Conclusion

Leading in 2024 demands rethinking many outdated assumptions from the past. By prioritizing inclusion, well-being, empowerment and purpose over command-and-control models, annual reviews or training geared towards individual stars, we can cultivate more adaptive, resilient and just organizations prepared to navigate disruption. Going forward, I am committed to developing the skills, mindsets and relationships needed to lead differently through empathy, care, decentralization and championing diversity from the top down. Overall, we must redefine leadership itself as an act of service, relationship-building and community-care rather than a role or title to solve our industry's pressing challenges and thrive in the decades ahead.

25

Chapter 4

The Power of Experience: Developing Proficiency in Leadership

In the world of leadership development, it is widely acknowledged that proficiency in leadership cannot be solely attained through reading books and attending training courses. While these resources provide valuable knowledge and insights, true mastery is achieved through real-life experiences and continuous practice.

In this chapter, we will explore six key areas of practice that are crucial for leaders to develop their skills: building a unifying vision, developing strategy, hiring and motivating the right people, focusing on results, fostering innovation, and leading themselves.

Building a Unifying Vision

A strong and compelling vision is the foundation of effective leadership. Leaders must be able to articulate a clear direction that inspires and motivates their team towards a common goal. This requires the ability to communicate the vision in a way that resonates with others, and to create a shared sense of purpose and meaning. Leaders who have developed proficiency in this area can rally their team around a common cause and create a sense of unity and collaboration.

Developing Strategy

Strategic thinking is a critical skill for leaders. It involves the ability to analyze complex situations, anticipate future trends, and make informed decisions that align with the overall vision. Proficient leaders are skilled in strategic planning, setting goals, and creating action plans that guide their team towards success. They are able to adapt their strategies in response to changing circumstances, ensuring that their team remains focused and effective in achieving desired outcomes.

Hiring and Motivating the Right People

Leadership is not a solo endeavor. It requires assembling a team of talented individuals who share the same values and are motivated to contribute their best efforts. Proficient leaders excel in identifying and attracting top talent, ensuring a diverse mix of skills and perspectives within their team. They also possess the ability to inspire and motivate their team members, fostering a positive and productive work environment that drives performance and growth.

Focusing on Results

One of the hallmarks of effective leadership is a relentless focus on achieving results. Proficient leaders set high standards and expectations for themselves and their team, and they hold themselves accountable for delivering on their commitments. They create a culture of excellence by establishing clear performance metrics, providing regular feedback, and recognizing and rewarding achievements. By prioritizing results, proficient leaders drive continuous improvement and ensure the success of their team and organization.

Fostering Innovation

Innovation is a crucial factor for staying ahead in today's rapidly changing business landscape. Proficient leaders foster a culture of innovation by encouraging creativity, embracing new ideas, and providing opportunities for experimentation and learning. They create an environment where team members feel safe to take risks and think outside the box, leading to breakthrough solutions and driving organizational growth.

Leading Themselves

Leadership begins with self-leadership. Proficient leaders understand the importance of personal growth and development. They continuously strive to enhance their own skills, knowledge, and self-awareness. They demonstrate authenticity, integrity, and resilience, serving as role models for their team. By effectively leading themselves, proficient leaders inspire trust and confidence in others, creating a positive and empowering work environment.

Conclusion

While reading books and attending training courses are valuable resources for leadership development, true proficiency is achieved through real-life experience and continuous practice. Leaders who focus on building a unifying vision, developing strategy, hiring and motivating the right people, focusing on results, fostering innovation, and leading themselves are more likely to develop the skills necessary for effective leadership. By incorporating these areas of practice into their professional journey, leaders can enhance their capabilities and drive success for themselves and their organizations.

32

Chapter 5

Cross-Silo Leadership: Connecting Experts to Create Value

In today's complex and rapidly changing business environment, companies need to leverage expertise and collaborate across organizational boundaries in order to capitalize on promising innovations and opportunities. However, breaking down silos is often challenging for leaders and employees naturally focus on vertical relationships within their own teams or business units.

Instead of relying solely on formal restructuring which can be costly and confusing, leaders should focus on four activities: 1) developing cultural brokers within the organization who excel at bridging different groups 2) encouraging open-ended questioning that explores others' viewpoints 3) actively perspective-taking to understand different ways of thinking and 4) broadening employees' networks to include more distant connections. By supporting these four activities, leaders can nurture what the authors call "interface collaboration" where connecting and learning across boundaries becomes second nature.

In this chapter, we will explore how leaders can promote cross-silo collaboration by engaging in activities that connect people across divides.

Developing Cultural Brokers

It is essential that you work to identify and develop cultural brokers - employees who are skilled relationship-builders across different internal groups or external partners. These boundary-spanning individuals excel at connecting experts from disparate parts of the organization or beyond.

Leaders should look for potential brokers who demonstrate curiosity, cognitive flexibility and high emotional intelligence. Rather than siloed thinking, cultural brokers tend to see interconnectivity and are comfortable operating in ambiguity. Leaders can encourage brokers by exposing them to different functions, clients and contexts to expand their perspectives. Rotation through diverse roles, inclusion in cross-functional initiatives and partnerships with external entities are valuable developmental experiences.

Sponsoring informal networking events where brokers can meet new contacts is another way to support their bridging capacity. Leaders should also publicly recognize the collaborative contributions of brokers through awards, promotions and compensation to reinforce this activity.

Promoting Open-Ended Inquiry

It is important to promote open-ended inquiry and curiosity across boundaries. Leaders can encourage employees to ask questions that genuinely explore others' viewpoints rather than just confirming existing assumptions.

For instance, when initiating a new partnership between internal groups or external partners, leaders could design sessions focused on understanding different perspectives before rushing to solutions. Asking questions like "What key assumptions differ between our groups?" and "What factors or constraints shape your viewpoint?" can uncover insights and prevent misalignments down the road.

Leaders should model open-ended inquiry themselves by admitting what they don't know and asking outsiders for input to broaden their perspective. They can also train employees in skills like active listening, empathy and inquiry-based dialogue. Rewarding substantive information gathering and adjustment of opinions based on what is learned will motivate the desired behavior.

Taking Different Perspectives

In addition to inquiry, try actively taking others' perspectives - putting oneself in another's shoes to understand how they see the world. Immersion experiences, role reversal exercises and simulations are ways leaders can encourage perspective-taking across silos.

For example, leaders could have R&D scientists shadow customer support reps to gain empathy for user challenges. Or rotate manufacturing engineers to the sales team to get exposed to client objectives. Managers should participate alongside direct reports in these exchanges and discuss the experience afterward to reinforce interest in different viewpoints.

Leaders can also use tools like stakeholder mapping to visualize economic, emotional and other factors shaping stakeholders' positions. Taking time to articulate others' reality expands employee mindsets beyond narrow functional concerns.

Broadening Networks

Finally, there is power in broad professional networks in helping employees gain new knowledge and relate to very different groups. Leaders should actively sponsor relationship-building with both close and distant contacts inside and outside the organization.

Tactics include making diverse introductions, supporting conference attendance or involvement in external associations and enabling short-term collaboration with other companies. Job rotation and special projects again provide networking opportunities. Alumni groups, mentorship circles and online communities are other avenues to broaden networks.

The goal is developing employees' comfort engaging and learning from people far outside their normal function or industry. When networking is prioritized and rewarded, connections multiply.

Conclusion

Breaking down silos is critical but often difficult in complex organizations. Leaders can enable cross-boundary collaboration by focusing on four activities: developing cultural brokers, promoting open inquiry, encouraging perspective-taking and broadening employee networks. This moves organizations from narrowly siloed thinking to genuinely exploring different viewpoints and connecting diverse expertise. While formal restructuring has limitations, leaders who support cultural shifts toward curiosity, empathy and broad connectivity can unlock interface collaboration, innovation and new value. Executives should concentrate on enabling these activities through training, incentives, networking opportunities and role modeling. With practice, relating and collaborating across boundaries can become second nature.

39

Chapter 6

Building Trust as a Leader: The Importance of Positive Relationships. Consistency, and Good Judgment

Trust is a critical component of effective leadership. When employees trust their leader, they are more engaged, productive, and committed to the organization's success. However, establishing trust can be challenging, especially for new leaders or those who have damaged relationships in the past. According to recent research, there are three key elements that leaders should focus on to build trust: positive relationships, consistency, and good judgment/expertise.

In this chapter, we will provide an overview of why trust matters in leadership, summarize the key findings from the research on the 3 elements of trust, and expound on each element by providing detailed examples and recommendations for leaders. Building trust requires ongoing effort, self-awareness, and commitment to modeling the 3 elements of trust in daily interactions and decisions. When leaders embody positive relationships, consistency, and good judgment, they create the foundation for a thriving, high-trust organization.

The Importance of Trust in Leadership

Before examining the specific ways leaders can build trust, it is essential to understand why trust matters so much in leadership. Trust is the foundation on which effective leadership is built, enabling collaboration, engagement, and organizational success. When trust is present, employees feel confident in their leader's competence, character, and ability to make sound decisions. They are more willing to take risks, be vulnerable, and share ideas. High-trust organizations see greater innovation, better execution, and more engaged cultures. Leaders who have the trust of their employees are able to inspire others to achieve ambitious goals.

Distrust has the opposite effect. Leaders who lack trust breed fear and uncertainty in their employees. Without trust, people disengage, become reluctant to take risks, and focus more on self-preservation than the good of the organization. Distrust often stems from inconsistent behavior, poor judgment, broken promises, and damaged relationships. Rebuilding trust once it has been lost is a major undertaking, requiring sincere effort and changed behavior over an extended time. That is why it is so vital for leaders to intentionally build a culture of trust from the outset through positive relationships, consistency, and good judgment.

The 3 Elements of Trust

Recent research aimed to identify the key drivers of trust in leadership by analyzing over 80,000 360-degree reviews of leaders. The findings revealed three elements that most directly impact how much a leader is trusted by employees:

1. Positive Relationships

2. Consistency

3. Good Judgment/Expertise

Leaders who were rated highly on all three qualities were much more likely to be trusted by their direct reports, peers, and other colleagues. Of the three elements, positive relationships had the greatest impact on overall trust and appeared to be foundational to the other two. When positive relationships were lacking, leader trust suffered most severely. Each of the elements contributes to building a culture of trust and should be fostered intentionally by leaders.

The remainder of this chapter will explore each of the 3 elements of trust in detail, providing examples and recommendations for how leaders can practically apply them.

Positive Relationships

The research found that positive relationships were the most important driver of overall leader trust. Employees are far more likely to trust leaders who have taken the time to establish positive, interpersonal relationships with them. Positive relationships are built through honest, open communication, actively listening, and taking a genuine interest in employees' lives and development.

Leaders who foster positive relationships:

- Make time for 1-on-1 meetings to understand employees' needs, goals, and concerns

- Express care and interest in employees' lives beyond the workplace

- Provide support during difficult times and challenges

- Give emotional support and encouragement

- Communicate openly and transparently about organizational issues and decisions

- Admit mistakes sincerely without blaming others

- Listen attentively without interrupting or judging

Examples of ways leaders can build positive relationships include:

- Starting meetings with personal check-ins

- Celebrating milestones in employees' lives like birthdays, marriages, or births

- Handwriting notes of encouragement or appreciation

- Making time for informal conversations before/after meetings

- Sharing meals together

- Volunteering together at charity events

- Remembering personal details employees have shared

Fostering positive relationships requires dedication and ongoing effort, but pays off exponentially in increased trust. Employees know immediately if a leader's interest in their well-being is genuine or not. Leaders must be sincere and consistent in cultivating positive relationships.

Consistency

In addition to positive relationships, leaders also build trust through consistency. Employees trust leaders who are dependable, stick to clear values, and followthrough consistently on promises. Consistency requires leaders to align their words with actions and avoid unpredictable or erratic behavior.

Ways leaders can demonstrate consistency:

- Set clear expectations and stick to them

- Establish and uphold organizational values

- Follow through on commitments reliably

- Make well-informed decisions aligned to goals and priorities

- Maintain composure during times of stress

- Behave according to a clear set of ethical standards

- Align words to actions - do what you say you will do

- Ensure accountability and fairness - no favoritism

- Be transparent about decision-making processes

Examples of consistent leadership behavior:

- Publishing a clear set of team goals at the start of a project and reporting regularly on progress

- Having a well-defined decision-making process for new ideas that is applied consistently

- Responding calmly and promptly during a crisis without overreacting

- Following through on a promise to investigate an employee's concern by the promised deadline

- Refusing to bend stated policies for one individual that would not apply to others

Leaders must examine their own behavior honestly to identify inconsistencies and seek feedback from others when needed. Staying disciplined under pressure is critical to maintaining consistency. While adaptability and flexibility are also important leadership qualities, they should not come at the expense of needed consistency. Employees trust leaders most when they know what to expect.

Good Judgment/Expertise

In addition to relationships and consistency, the research indicated that leaders who demonstrate good judgment and expertise inspire higher trust. Employees rely on leaders who possess sound wisdom and demonstrate expertise in their roles. Good judgment enables leaders to assess situations astutely and make wise, data-driven decisions. Expertise results from strong capabilities, experience, and competence in a leader's field.

Ways leaders exhibit good judgment:

- Thinking critically to avoid rushed, overly emotional, or biased decisions

- Considering multiple perspectives and identifying key considerations before deciding

- Admitting when they need more expertise and involving others wisely

- Identifying possible unintended consequences of decisions

- Balancing risks and opportunities appropriately

- Applying past experience and lessons learned to navigate new situations

Examples of expertise in leadership roles:

- Having a strong knowledge base in the organization's industry

- Understanding the technical skills needed for the organization's success

- Possessing experience managing budgets and finances wisely if in an executive role

- Having sharp strategic planning and data analysis capabilities

- Applying strong communication, coaching, and facilitation skills

- Demonstrating creative problem solving and project management abilities

Conclusion

Trust is the foundation for productive, engaging workplaces. According to comprehensive research, positive relationships, consistency, and good judgment are the three qualities that build trust most effectively in leadership roles. Leaders must dedicate focused effort to cultivating trust through exhibiting these qualities authentically and continuously. When leaders have trusting relationships with employees, organizations thrive. By living out the 3 elements of trust - positive relationships, consistency, and good judgment - leaders can transform their organizations by inspiring engagement, innovation, and shared success. The rewards of high-trust leadership are immense, but require commitment and courage. The effort is well worth the substantial benefits to individuals, teams, and organizations.

51

Chapter 7

Great Leaders Are Thoughtful and Deliberate, Not Impulsive and Reactive

Effective leadership requires self-awareness and emotional regulation. All leaders have two sides of themselves - the rational, thoughtful self that makes considered choices, and the impulsive, reactive self driven by raw emotion. Great leaders recognize these two selves, observe them in real-time, and make deliberate choices to respond from their thoughtful, rational side, rather than reactively.

This allows great leaders to be in control of themselves and the situation, rather than controlled by their emotions. Great leaders notice their emotions, question their assumptions, and take responsibility for their behaviors. By doing so, they can avoid impulsive overreactions and poor decisions that undermine their leadership.

The Two Selves

Within every leader are two selves - the rational self and the impulsive self:

The Rational Self: This self is controlled by the prefrontal cortex, the part of the brain responsible for rational thinking and decision making. When operating from this self, a leader is measured, thoughtful, and capable of making deliberate choices. Their actions come from a place of reason rather than raw emotion.

The Impulsive Self: This self is controlled by the amygdala, the part of the brain responsible for emotional reactions. When operating from this self, a leader is reactive, rash, and frustrated. Their actions come from a place of impulse rather than reason.

Recognizing the Two Selves in Real Time

The key is for leaders to recognize when these two selves show up in real-time situations. This self-awareness allows leaders to consciously choose how to respond.

There are several indicators that can help a leader identify when their impulsive self is taking over:

- Strong negative emotions arising, like impatience, frustration, or anger

- A compulsion to dig in one's heels and defend their position

- An absolute conviction that they are right

- An urge to take immediate action based on their emotions

Strategies for Responding Deliberately

Once a leader notices their impulsive self showing up, they can employ strategies to engage their rational self and respond deliberately:

- *Label the Emotions*: Putting a name to the emotions creates psychological distance and self-control.

Recognizing "I am feeling impatient" rather than just feeling impatience allows a leader to reflect before reacting.

- *Watch for Stubbornness*: Noticing an instinct to dig in heels or defend a position indicates the impulsive self trying to take over. A leader can pause and consider other perspectives.

- *Ask "What Else Could Be True?"*: This question counteracts the tendency towards confirmation bias when the impulsive self takes over. By considering other perspectives, a leader can respond rationally.

- *Take Responsibility*: Rather than blaming others, a leader can reflect on their own responsibility in the situation and focus on what they can control - their own behavior and response.

Examples of Thoughtful Leadership

Consider a few examples that demonstrate how great leaders recognize their two selves and respond deliberately:

- *Diffusing Employee Frustration*: When an employee expresses anger about a new policy, a reactive leader may become defensive and dig in their heels. A thoughtful leader pauses, recognizes their own rising frustration, and calmly listens to understand the employee's perspective. They then explain the rationale for the policy change without judgment.

- *Handling Critical Feedback*: Upon receiving negative feedback, an impulsive leader might lash out at the critic or dismiss the feedback entirely. A thoughtful leader breathes through the initial emotional reaction, thanks the critic, and reflects on what there is to learn from the perspective.

- *Controlling Impatience*: As a deadline approaches, a leader may feel rising panic and urgency. A reactive leader expresses impatience by pressuring the team. A thoughtful leader notices their anxiety, reframes the urgency as enthusiasm, and motivates the team positively.

Conclusion

By developing self-awareness and the capacity to recognize their two selves in real-time, leaders can respond thoughtfully and deliberately, rather than impulsively and reactively. Key practices include noticing emotions, watching for stubbornness, questioning assumptions, and taking responsibility. With reflection and experience, great leaders strengthen their ability to override their impulses and act rationally for the greater good. This thoughtful leadership builds credibility, earns respect, and drives results.

Chapter 8

Ethical Leadership: Building Trust Through Principled Actions

In today's corporate environment, business leaders face immense pressure to deliver results and boost profits. However, the ethical misconduct of leaders is an increasingly prevalent concern. Recent corporate scandals such as Enron and Theranos demonstrate how an obsessive focus on success can lead executives down an unethical path. More than ever, leaders need to focus on building trust and leading with integrity.

Leaders should exercise caution, take calculated risks, adhere to principles, avoid the "fun boss" mentality, maintain professional distance from employees, and practice self-awareness. By embracing ethical leadership strategies, executives can earn the trust of their teams and the public.

Leading with Caution and Calculated Risks

Showing caution and taking calculated risks helps leaders gain trust. In a competitive business climate, leaders may feel pressure to take excessive risks to get ahead. However, leaders need to thoughtfully assess risks and potential ethical implications before moving forward. As Amy Edmondson, Novartis Professor of Leadership and Management at Harvard Business School, advises, leaders should create a psychologically safe environment where employees feel comfortable voicing concerns about potential risks. By encouraging transparent conversations about risks, leaders can make more informed decisions. Calculated risks that thoughtfully weigh benefits and potential downsides are preferable to impulsive gambles. Adhering to processes for ethical decision-making can provide helpful guardrails. With cautious and deliberative risk-taking, leaders demonstrate good judgment and responsibility.

Upholding Principles and Organizational Values

In addition to cautious risk analysis, adherence to principles is a key element of ethical leadership. Leaders build trust when they consistently uphold ethical principles and organizational values. Actions speak louder than words. If leaders espouse integrity yet tacitly condone questionable practices, they breed cynicism among employees. Leaders need to embody the values they tout through their everyday decisions and conduct. They should hold themselves and employees accountable to living up to stated principles. This requires addressing ethical gray areas head on rather than avoiding difficult conversations. According to leadership experts, grounding decisions in core values provides a moral compass when dilemmas arise. Leaders who demonstrate commitment to doing the right thing signal that profits do not eclipse principles.

Avoiding the "Fun Boss" Mentality

Leaders should also avoid the temptation to try and be the "fun boss" to gain approval. The fun boss mentality prioritizes being liked over making sound leadership decisions. Leaders who try too hard to be friends with employees may have difficulty making objective personnel decisions. They may lack necessary professional boundaries with their teams. As Yahoo CEO Marissa Mayer exemplified, leadership isn't a popularity contest. Leaders need to focus on driving results, developing employees, and making principled calls—not on being the cool boss. That said, leaders should avoid coming across as authoritarian. Respect and accessibility are important. Leaders can take a participative leadership approach where employees are actively engaged in decision-making. Ultimately, ethical leaders aim for a balance where they are appreciated and respected but maintain professional objectivity.

Keeping Professional Distance

Related to avoiding the "fun boss" pitfall, leaders need to maintain professional distance from employees. Getting too close or informal with employees can cloud objectivity and breed inappropriate fraternization. Leaders need to be friendly but not friends. Small talk in the hallway is fine, but happy hour drinks after work tend to cross the line. Work gatherings, like holiday parties, present pitfalls that require vigilance. Harassment issues can emerge when booze lowers inhibitions. Leaders should act professionally at all times, on and off the clock. If traveling for business, prudent leaders meet in public spaces versus alone in a hotel room with colleagues. In the #MeToo era, leaders ignore boundaries at their own peril. Lawsuits or scandal can ensue. While leaders should be accessible, keeping appropriate professional distance fosters trust and respect.

Practicing Greater Self-Awareness

Finally, self-awareness is essential to ethical leadership. Self-aware leaders recognize their own biases and tendencies to rationalize or behave unethically under pressure. They reflect on past missteps to strengthen moral muscles for the future. Many corporate scandals tie back to oblivious or self-aggrandizing leaders. Events like Enron underscore the dangers of hubristic, conflict-ridden leaders who lack self-control. To avoid such pitfalls, executives need to cultivate humility and introspection. They should solicit candid feedback from trusted advisors. Surrounding themselves with diverse viewpoints surfaces blind spots. Self-aware leaders also need work-life balance and confidants beyond the office to provide perspective. Practicing self-awareness and self-care enables leaders to stay centered amid turbulence.

Conclusion

Executives face growing demands to lead ethically and build trust in turbulent times. Leaders can earn confidence by exhibiting caution, adhering to principles, avoiding the "fun boss" trap, maintaining professionalism, and developing self-awareness. Leading by example and putting people over profits ultimately wins trust. Ethics and success do not have to be mutually exclusive. With mindful, values-based leadership, executives can steer their organizations in an ethical direction.

The future needs leaders who look beyond the bottom line and aim higher on the moral compass.

Chapter 9

Navigating Strategic Ambiguity: Three Approaches for Effective Management

In today's fast-paced and ever-changing business environment, it's not uncommon for companies and units to face situations where their strategy is unclear, in flux, or constantly evolving. This lack of clarity can create challenges for managers who are tasked with leading their teams to success.

However, the best managers are able to rise above the uncertainty and provide steady, realistic direction while leading with excellence.

In this chapter, we will explore three approaches that managers can use to navigate strategic ambiguity and achieve success even when the strategy isn't clear.

Take Pragmatic Action

One of the most effective ways to manage strategic ambiguity is to take pragmatic action. This involves getting back to basics and focusing on delivering value to the organization. By taking a back-to-basics approach, managers can establish a solid foundation for their team's work, even when the overall strategy is unclear. This can involve identifying key performance indicators (KPIs), streamlining processes, and focusing on the things that matter most to the organization.

Another important aspect of taking pragmatic action is placing intelligent bets on what you do know. This involves making informed decisions based on the information that is available, rather than waiting for clarity on the overall strategy. By making informed decisions, managers can help their teams stay focused and motivated, even when the bigger picture is unclear.

Managers can embrace short-term strategies by operating in sprints. This involves breaking down larger goals into smaller, more manageable tasks, and focusing on delivering results in short, focused bursts. By operating in sprints, managers can help their teams stay focused and motivated, while also delivering valuable outcomes to the organization.

Cultivate Emotional Steadiness

In addition to taking pragmatic action, managers can cultivate emotional steadiness in themselves and their teams. This involves being aware of the situation and acknowledging and navigating their emotions. By being aware of their emotions, managers can better manage their own reactions to ambiguity and uncertainty, and help their teams do the same.

Another important aspect of cultivating emotional steadiness is keeping team communication open. This involves creating a safe and supportive environment where team members feel comfortable sharing their thoughts and concerns. By keeping communication open, managers can help their teams stay informed and engaged, even when the strategy is unclear.

Managers can learn more about the situation by seeking out information and insights from others. This can involve talking to colleagues, seeking out expert advice, and staying up-to-date on industry trends and developments. By seeking out information and insights, managers can gain a better understanding of the situation and make more informed decisions.

Tap into Others' Expertise

The third approach for managing strategic ambiguity is to tap into others' expertise. This involves imagining what the leader you respect the most would do, engaging other managers, and embracing the wisdom of thought leaders. By seeking out the advice and insights of others, managers can gain a fresh perspective on the situation and identify new opportunities for growth and success.

One way to tap into others' expertise is to engage other managers in the organization. This can involve seeking out their advice, sharing best practices, and collaborating on projects and initiatives. By engaging other managers, managers can gain a better understanding of the organization's overall strategy and how their team fits into it.

Another way to tap into others' expertise is to embrace the wisdom of thought leaders. This involves seeking out the insights and advice of experts in the field, and applying their principles and practices to your own work. By embracing the wisdom of thought leaders, managers can gain a deeper understanding of the latest trends and developments in their industry, and identify new opportunities for growth and success.

Conclusion

Managing strategic ambiguity is a critical skill for managers in today's fast-paced and ever-changing business environment. By taking pragmatic action, cultivating emotional steadiness, and tapping into others' expertise, managers can lead their teams to success even when the strategy isn't clear. By embracing these approaches, managers can turn uncertainty into an opportunity for growth and innovation, and help their organizations thrive in a rapidly changing world. By developing the skills and mindset necessary to navigate strategic ambiguity, managers can confidently lead their teams into the unknown, and achieve great success in the face of uncertainty.

Chapter 10

Shaping Decisions: The Nuanced Reality of CEO Decision-Making

The common perception is that CEOs are the ultimate decision makers in their companies, personally involved in and responsible for every major choice. However, research shows that this is a myth. While CEOs do provide executive guidance, they do not make most decisions directly. Rather, their role involves shaping the decision-making process.

In this chapter, we will explore the key arguments around why the view of CEO-as-decision-maker is a myth, and provide more detail into the nuanced reality of a CEO's decision-making responsibilities.

The Reality of CEO Decision-Making

The main thrust of the argument is that CEOs do not actually make most substantive business decisions directly. There are three main reasons for this:

1. The shear breadth of decisions required across a company makes it impossible for one person to decide everything. A CEO must rely on delegation and processes that engage the appropriate experts.

2. Direct decision-making is an inefficient use of a CEO's limited time and attention. Their time is better spent providing high-level guidance and making selective interventions when needed.

3. Overreaching into specific decisions can undermine a CEO's ability to monitor objectively and maintain a broad perspective.

Rather than constantly deciding, CEOs focus their efforts on shaping decisions by designing processes to leverage the full organization, choosing when to provide direct input, and monitoring execution to identify needed adjustments. This selective engagement across the organization's decision-making is a more effective approach aligned to the CEO's role.

Examples of Shaping Decisions Indirectly

To provide more specific illustration, CEOs shape organizational decisions in a few key ways:

Delegation and Processes

A CEO must determine what types of decisions can be fully delegated vs. those that require some CEO-level input. Delegation empowers managers and utilizes expertise across the company efficiently.

An example is a technology company assigning product feature prioritization to the head of product management, trusting her domain expertise. While the CEO monitors progress, she does not decide the product roadmap herself.

The CEO also designs processes bringing the right internal stakeholders together for larger decisions. This facilitates buy-in and high-quality decisions benefiting from diverse inputs.

An example is a CEO establishing a cross-functional committee including sales, marketing, and product heads to decide pricing for a new offering. Rather than decide pricing alone, the CEO created a process relying on the combined insights of the committee.

Selective Intervention

Rather than constant top-down decisions, CEOs aim to provide input selectively when their involvement adds value. This selective intervention provides guidance while avoiding undermining delegation.

For example, a CEO may choose to weigh in on a particular acquisition target but not on the details of negotiation strategy, which he delegates to the VP of Business Development. This balances delegation with the CEO leveraging his knowledge of the target to inform strategy.

Monitoring and Adjustment

CEOs further shape decisions by monitoring progress on delegated choices and intervening with adjustments or course corrections as needed. If execution veers off track, the CEO has responsibility to recognize gaps and ensure realignment.

For instance, a CEO entrusted her head of sales to develop a new reseller strategy. Upon monitoring early results, she noticed a disconnect between sales incentives and reseller program goals. She worked with the sales lead to adjust incentive structures to better align with the intended strategy. Her oversight identified a needed adjustment to ensure execution.

Conclusion

While CEOs do make some direct choices, the notion of the CEO as the ultimate decider for a company is largely a myth. The scale and complexity of modern enterprises means CEOs must enable decision-making across the organization through smart delegation, institutional processes, selective input, and active monitoring. This empowers others and makes the CEO's involvement more effective when focused on shaping the most crucial decisions. The image of the CEO making authoritative choices on all matters is outdated, replaced by the reality of enabling good decisions across the entire company.

BUILDING HIGH-PERFORMING ORGANIZATIONS

Chapter 11

Leading the Creative Process: Supporting Innovation While Maintaining Business Success

Creativity is invaluable for any organization, but managing creative teams comes with unique challenges. Creative work is intensely personal, driven by intrinsic motivations and a process that is difficult to control or dictate. At the same time, businesses must deliver successful outcomes and profits. How can leaders empower creativity while meeting the practical needs of running a business?

In this chapter, we will explore how to effectively lead creative teams.

Understanding the Creative Process

The first step to leading creative teams is understanding how the creative process works. Creativity is not just about the final product; it is a journey that involves the mindset, motivations, and approach of creative individuals. As a leader, you need to grasp the full depth of this process in order to nurture innovation.

Start by scheduling regular one-on-one check-ins with your creative staff. Have open-ended conversations to understand how they work through challenges, find inspiration, and approach projects. Ask thoughtful questions and listen intently to their responses. Avoid interrogating them; the goal is to foster trust and open dialogue. With time, you will gain insight into the creative process for each individual on your team.

You may notice patterns in the techniques your team uses to spark ideas, such as brainstorming, researching, or experiential activities like museum visits. Be open-minded; every creative professional has a unique way of accessing inspiration.

Your check-ins will also shed light on when and where they feel most productive. Many designers and writers prefer working from home, while others thrive in a bustling studio. Store this knowledge and use it to tailor your management approach.

The better you comprehend the creative journey, the better you can nurture innovation and avoid impeding the artistic process. Freedom and space are critical for creativity to flourish.

Providing Space for Creativity

With a firm understanding of your team's process, you can take steps to foster rather than fetter creativity. One of the biggest mistakes leaders make is trying to control the creative process. Strict rules and micromanagement stifle talent and innovation. Instead, adopt a decentralized management approach that gives creatives freedom.

Encourage creative problem-solving by presenting challenges or desired outcomes rather than detailed instructions. Set necessary constraints, like budget parameters, but beyond that, give your team space. Allow creatives to experiment, make mistakes, and organically develop solutions. Intervene only if they veer drastically off track.

Be flexible about logistics like schedules, work environments, and collaboration styles. Meetings are notorious creativity killers, so limit required meetings and let creatives work when and where they are most productive. Support individual work or small-group work sessions as needed. Autonomy and flexibility will allow innovation to flourish.

You are there to provide high-level guidance, resources, and constructive feedback. But you must let your team take ownership of the creative process itself. Micromanaging their work will only lead to frustration, low morale, and mediocre results. As long as your creatives are working effectively towards the desired goals, give them space to do it their way.

Giving Constructive Feedback

While creative autonomy is crucial, leaders still need to oversee work and provide feedback. Constructive criticism is essential, but delivery is key. Thoughtlessly delivered feedback can deter creativity instead of improving it.

First, make feedback a regular part of your check-ins, not just a final review. Early feedback allows for iteration and growth rather than forcing a last-minute change of direction. Second, give feedback thoughtfully. Comment respectfully on the work itself, not the creator's ability or talent. Frame critiques as constructive suggestions to consider rather than strict directives. Listen to your team member's perspectives before deciding on changes.

When giving critical feedback, begin with affirmation. Highlight the strong aspects of their work before offering critique. Balance criticism with praise. Remember, your role is to inspire, not control. Phrase feedback as a proposed way to improve, not a demand.

Finally, focus feedback on the objectives of the work rather than trying to impose your personal creative vision. Providing structure and direction is reasonable, but avoid dictating taste. You want to develop your team's skills, not stamp out their creative identity. With care and practice, you can deliver constructive feedback that empowers creatives.

Facilitating Collaboration

While creative work requires space for individual contributions, cross-functional collaboration is also essential. Creative products must align with business needs and technical capabilities. Encourage your creative team to regularly connect with other departments like marketing, production, and sales.

Start by educating each team on the other's perspective. Provide information about goals, resources, and constraints in other departments. Have creatives sit in on production meetings, let marketers review product designs firsthand. Greater familiarity will help align priorities and workflows.

Design collaboration into projects from the start. Bring creative, technical, and business leads together during the planning process. Facilitate brainstorms, project summits, and informal workshops. Collaboration should shape ideas from conception rather than critiquing work after the fact.

Role clarity is also key; each collaborator should understand their contributions and responsibilities. Confusion over ownership leads to mistakes and frustration. Clearly define roles for concept development, execution, approvals, and testing. Build shared purpose through collective brainstorms and presenting cross-department feedback.

With trust, communication, and clarity of roles, you can facilitate seamless collaboration between creatives and other departments. Aligned priorities plus specialized contributions will lead to inspired solutions.

Balancing Innovation and Business Needs

The tension between creativity and practical business needs is eternal. As a leader, you must strike a balance, neither sacrificing business viability for innovation nor missing opportunities due to rigid risk-aversion.

First, articulate the value creative solutions can bring, whether delighting customers, reaching new audiences, or streamlining processes. Understand that creativity sometimes requires experimentation and short-term resource investments to generate significant long-term gains. Make the case for promising creative projects even if they carry risks and uncertainties.

At the same time, identify non-negotiable business constraints. Be transparent about budget limitations, deadlines, target metrics, and other practical boundaries within which your team must innovate. Creative aspirations cannot undermine business viability. Contextualize how your team's innovations fit into the broader organization and its success.

When evaluating and implementing creative ideas, undertake reasonable due diligence. REQUEST that your team gather customer feedback, conduct user tests, and research adoption by target markets. REQUIRE feasible implementation plans with resource needs and risk assessments. Judiciously investing in vetting and perfecting creative concepts will pay dividends.

With open communication and responsible innovation practices, creative solutions can be implemented successfully. By conveying the value of creativity while requiring diligence, leaders empower innovation that moves the business forward.

Conclusion

Fostering creativity presents unique leadership challenges that require understanding your team's process, providing ample autonomy, delivering thoughtful feedback, facilitating collaboration, and balancing innovation with practical business needs. Adopt a supportive rather than directive approach. Embrace creativity's unpredictability and trust your team's talents. With the right environment and guidance, they will deliver inspired, business-relevant solutions that drive growth and success. By implementing the strategies outlined here, leaders can effectively direct creative teams to new heights.

Part 2

Career Development

Chapter 12

Navigating Feelings of Confidence and Self-Doubt After a Promotion

Moving into a higher-level leadership role is an exciting opportunity, but it can also spur complicated emotions. Promotions are usually based on past performance, so it's natural to feel confident that your skills will carry into the new role. However, most promotions also require developing new capabilities on the job. This contrast can make your confidence waver at times or even tip into self-doubt. How can you find the right balance?

In this chapter, we will explore strategies on navigating feelings of confidence and self-doubt after a promotion.

The Optimal Level of Confidence After a Promotion

Leadership transitions require just the right amount of confidence - not too much and not too little. Overconfidence early on can make you resistant to feedback and blind to developing new skills. However, underconfidence promotes indecisiveness and inhibits you from fully stepping into your new role. The optimal approach lies between these extremes. You must balance confidence in your abilities with humility to continue growing. Here are some best practices:

- Remind yourself that you were promoted for good reason. Reflect on the strengths that got you here and how they apply in your new role. This boosts confidence.

- Don't get overly attached to past accomplishments. Remain open and eager to gain new skills. This balances confidence with humility.

- When you make mistakes, see them as opportunities to improve rather than just failures. This prevents dips in confidence.

- Ask trusted advisors for honest feedback on your performance. Use their input to calibrate your self-perception. This provides reality checks on confidence.

Adjusting Your Mindset About Confidence

Making this mental shift starts with changing your mindset about confidence. View it as something you intentionally adjust, not as fixed or dependent on outside validation. Give yourself permission to move up and down on the spectrum of confidence as you tackle new challenges. Here are some mindset tips:

- Don't beat yourself up for some self-doubt - it's inevitable early on. Focus on building confidence through preparation and practice.

- Remember that no one expects you to know everything on day one. Have a learning mindset rather than needing to prove yourself.

- Focus more on confidence in your ability to learn rather than confidence that you already have all the answers. The latter is unrealistic.

- Imagine yourself succeeding in difficult leadership situations. This visualization can boost confidence.

Managing Imposter Syndrome

One of the biggest confidence killers for new leaders is imposter syndrome - feeling like a fraud who doesn't deserve the promotion. This is incredibly common. Try these strategies to manage imposter syndrome:

- Identify triggering situations for imposter syndrome and prepare extra hard for them. Over-preparation breeds confidence.
- Keep a file of positive feedback and accomplishments. Re-read it when you feel like a fraud.
- Reframe feelings of fraudulence as humility. They show you want to do a good job.
- Share feelings of self-doubt with a mentor. Their reassurance can restore confidence.

Seeking Feedback from Others

Getting objective feedback from others helps calibrate your confidence. It highlights both strengths and blind spots. Here's how to do it effectively:

- Ask for feedback often early on - weekly if possible. This helps confidence keep pace with your actual performance.

- Seek input from those who see different aspects of your new role - direct reports, peers, superiors.

- Pose specific questions about your leadership capabilities. Vague questions elicit useless responses.

- Clarify next steps based on feedback. This shows you're taking it seriously.

- Thank people for their candor. This encourages ongoing honesty.

Benchmarking Your Progress

Finally, benchmark your skills and confidence against the learning curves of other new leaders. Remember that some self-doubt, knowledge gaps, and mistakes are normal at first. Tie confidence to your progress mastering the role, not immediate perfection. Useful benchmarks include:

- Feedback from veterans on how long it took them to gain their footing

- Written goals and training plans that outline skill development timelines

- Metrics that demonstrate your leadership impact over time

Conclusion

A promotion brings deserved confidence along with natural self-doubt. Finding the right balance requires adjusting your mindset, managing imposter syndrome, seeking frequent feedback, and benchmarking progress. With this approach, newly promoted leaders can land on an optimal confidence level, empowering their transition. Though some uncertainty is inevitable at first, you will gain your footing faster by utilizing the strategies in this chapter.

Chapter 13

Making Learning a Daily Habit for Career Success

In today's ever-changing career landscape, the ability to continuously learn and adapt is more important than ever before. As the provided text by the authors highlights, careers are becoming increasingly "squiggly" - with more frequent role changes and fluid development in new directions. To thrive in this environment, developing the capacity for ongoing learning is vital. Adaptive, lifelong learners are invaluable assets to organizations. By making learning a consistent, daily habit, we can increase our readiness for new opportunities, build resilience for inevitable challenges, and take charge of our long-term career success.

In this chapter, we will explore how to make learning a seamless part of our everyday work and lives. The long-term dividends for our careers will be invaluable.

Making Time for Focused Learning

The first technique is to create dedicated time for focused learning every day. With the busyness of most schedules, learning is often pushed aside. By deliberately blocking off time, even just 30 minutes per day, we can make space for concentration on acquiring new skills and knowledge.

For example, allocating the first 30 minutes of your workday to focused learning can help you start each day proactively. You could utilize this time to read industry publications to stay on top of trends in your field, take an online tutorial to build technical skills, or curate a reading list of books and articles for professional development. Establishing learning time as part of your morning routine makes it more likely it will actually happen, compared to trying to fit it in ad hoc during the day.

Similarly, setting aside 30-60 minutes in the evening for learning activities can be worthwhile. Uninterrupted evening learning time could involve more intensive online courses, listening to educational podcasts during your commute, taking notes on books related to your career aims, researching ideas and innovations in your industry, and more. Blocking off focused learning at the beginning and end of your day helps sandwich other priorities and make learning a consistent habit.

Integrating Microlearning into Daily Tasks

In addition to focused learning sessions, integrate microlearning activities throughout your day. Microlearning involves short, bite-sized learning in the midst of other tasks. This technique allows for learning in small increments, as opposed to lengthy concentrated study. With deliberate effort, microlearning can be injected into routine daily activities.

For example, while commuting you could listen to a short 5-10 minute podcast on a skill you want to develop. Over your lunch break, you might spend 10 minutes reading an article that gives tips for improving a challenging area of your work. When washing dishes or folding laundry at home, you could listen to a microlesson on building your capabilities as a leader or manager. Even just 5 minutes of reading here or there during the day adds up over time.

Microlearning works best when the content is directly relevant in the moment. Think about the tasks you engage in each day and identify microlearning opportunities that will provide timely knowledge. With practice, integrating bite-sized learning into your routine daily activities becomes second nature.

Leveraging Everyday Interactions for Peer Learning

Informal peer learning through everyday human interactions is another opportunity highlighted by the authors. Connecting with colleagues at work and contacts in your broader network for short conversations centered on exchanging knowledge and insights can be quite valuable over time.

For example, use lunch, coffee breaks, or pre-meeting chatter as a chance to ask peers about an approach they use that you want to learn more about, or discuss innovations and new learning in your field. Treat meetings as opportunities to solicit advice and perspectives from colleagues on challenges you're facing or ideas you want to develop. Schedule brief phone calls with your wider network to learn about their career journeys and lessons learned. When conversations turn to non-work topics, steer discussions back to professional development issues where peers may have experience to share.

In the course of day-to-day interaction at work and within your network, exchanges that facilitate peer learning can become habitual. As long as conversations are kept focused and respectful of others' time, brief peer learning opportunities integrated into your routine activities can deliver compounded knowledge over the long-term.

Prioritizing Reflection for Continuous Improvement

Finally, carve out time for self-reflection on a consistent basis. Reflecting on your learning helps synthesize new knowledge and identify personal growth opportunities. Setting aside as little as 5-10 minutes per day for focused reflection can lead to important realizations that drive continuous improvement.

One approach is to block off reflection time late in the afternoon or early evening when your mind is less pressured. Use this time to look back on your learning from the day and think about how your new knowledge or skills could be applied. Journal in writing or audio record your reflections on questions like: What am I learning that is making me stretch and grow? What knowledge gaps has today's learning revealed that I should address? How can I put today's learning into practice for better work outcomes? How does today's learning relate to my career goals?

Prioritizing regular reflection helps cement new lessons learned, while identifying ongoing learning needs to drive your continued growth and development. Over time, reflection at the end of each day to shape plans for the next day can become routine best practice.

Conclusion

In today's fluid career environment, the capacity to continually learn, unlearn and relearn is more vital than ever. By adopting the techniques recommended by the authors, such as focused daily learning sessions, microlearning integrated into routine tasks, informal peer exchanges, and daily reflection, learning can become a habitual part of our work and lives. Making learning a consistent behavior yields compounding benefits over our careers. While it requires deliberate effort to make time for learning each day, the long-term dividends make it a worthy investment. Start putting these tips into practice to take charge of your ongoing professional development and career success.

Chapter 14

Overcoming the Midlife Crisis: Causes, Timing, and Strategies for Moving Forward

The so-called "midlife crisis" is a phenomenon familiar to many adults. Middle-aged people across all careers and lifestyles can unexpectedly find themselves grappling with feelings of dissatisfaction, regret, or a desire for radical change. This struggle often comes as a surprise following decades spent building careers, wealth, families, and stability. While a midlife crisis can be painful and disruptive, it does not have to lead to drastic life upheaval. By understanding the potential causes, timing, and productive strategies for navigating it, individuals can overcome this challenge and rediscover meaning and fulfillment.

Causes of the Midlife Crisis

The midlife crisis does not stem from any single cause but rather a convergence of factors that tend to arise for many adults in their late 30s through 50s. These include:

- *Awareness of mortality.* In youth, people often feel invincible. Approaching midlife, the realization sets in that death is inevitable. This can trigger urgent questions about whether one is spending time meaningfully.

- *Discontent with life accomplishments.* Many experience dissatisfaction upon comparing their lives to expectations, feeling they have not achieved enough status, wealth, or recognition.

- *Stagnation.* Some find themselves in a routine, no longer learning or taking on new challenges. Even comfortable ruts can breed restlessness over time.

- *Comparisons with others.* With peers at similar life stages, there are more cues to compare accomplishments and youthful aspirations to reality. This can reveal a distressing gap.

- *Shifting priorities.* Values often evolve with age, away from competition and individualism toward deeper fulfillment. This change is not always conscious but can undermine former goals.

- *Identity loss.* Younger adults often define themselves by title, appearance, role, or external pursuits. In midlife, such focal points of identity may lose importance, requiring internal redefinition.

- *Marriage or relationship issues.* Marital struggles, infidelity, or divorce rates peak from ages 40 to 44. This instability can fuel a crisis.

The midlife crisis often results from the collision between youthful expectations and middle-aged realities. As perspectives shift with maturity and age, regret, desire for change, and questioning of identity and purpose can surge.

Why the Midlife Crisis Timing?

If the above causes can arise at any age, why does this crisis tend to strike during middle adulthood? Some key factors converge in midlife that can trigger this phenomenon:

- Physical aging becomes noticeable, reminding one of fading youth and mortality.

- Milestone ages like 40 and 50 provide natural points for life evaluation.

- Most have been in careers or relationships long enough to achieve stability or start feeling restlessness.

- Financial independence and security often peak, providing the means to consider major life changes.

- With children grown or almost there, some feel a void regarding purpose.

- Hormonal changes physically reinforce tendencies toward introspection and unease.

In addition to the causes outlined earlier, these dynamics of midlife explain the common timing of the midlife crisis between roughly 40 and 60 years old. It is a period prone to profound reevaluation of priorities and meaning.

Strategies for Moving Forward

While painful, a midlife crisis can provide an opportunity to rediscover passion and joy. The key is to navigate it constructively. Strategies include:

- *Reflect meaningfully on goals and values.* Look for misalignment between your current life and evolving priorities. Set aside what no longer motivates you.

- *Reconnect with purpose.* Identify activities and roles that provide a sense of meaning, especially helping others. Seek small ways to build these into daily life.

- *Seek new challenges.* Break up monotony by learning new skills, taking intellectually engaging classes, or pursuing creative projects. Replace stagnation with empowering growth.

- *Focus less on achievement comparison.* Avoid excessive reflection on status or wealth. Comparison breeds discontent. Refocus on your own growth and meaning.

- *Communicate with loved ones.* Confide constructively in family and friends for perspective. Seek their support in making positive changes.

- *Pursue counseling.* Therapists can provide objective guidance. Address underlying issues fueling your crisis.

- *Make gradual changes.* Avoid radical upheaval. Slowly incorporate fulfilling pursuits and modify unfulfilling areas of life.

- *Practice mindfulness and gratitude.* Notice and appreciate each moment. This calms anxiety about past regrets and future mortality.

With thoughtful effort, the midlife crisis can be transformed into an opportunity for positive growth and renewal. Set aside stagnation and superficial pursuits. Redirect energy toward what provides meaning - your values, passions, and service to others. Small mindset and lifestyle adjustments add up to profound changes. You have the power to design a life aligned with your maturing priorities.

Conclusion

A midlife crisis can strike the most successful, shaking assumptions about career, relationships, and purpose. But it need not lead to despair or reckless life upheaval. Though often triggered by feelings of mortality, stagnation, and questioning of accomplishment or identity, it can motivate those experiencing it to rediscover meaning. Reflection, renewed purpose, challenging growth, and gradual change enable moving forward. With this constructive approach, the midlife crisis becomes no crisis at all, but instead a pathway to a revitalized life.

BUILDING HIGH-PERFORMING ORGANIZATIONS

Chapter 15

Taking Control of Your Career Development When Your Company Won't

In an ideal world, companies would invest substantial time and resources into developing their employees' careers. Unfortunately, that is often not the reality. Many organizations today are focused on short-term goals and quick returns, leaving little room for employee career development. This puts the onus on individuals to take charge of bettering their own skills and experiences if they want to advance professionally.

While it's understandable to feel frustrated with a lack of organizational support, it is still possible to thrive in your career - even when your company doesn't seem to care. By taking matters into your own hands, being proactive, and getting creative, you can find ways to build the knowledge, abilities, and connections that will fuel your professional growth.

Understanding What You're Evaluated On

The first strategy is to understand what your company genuinely values and seeks in employees when making promotion and compensation decisions. This may require some sleuthing if formal criteria are not clearly laid out. Talk to your manager and ask what specific skills, results, and behaviors they look for. Observe patterns in who climbs the ladder fastest in your workplace. Look at past job descriptions for higher-level roles you aspire to someday.

Once you identify the key areas your workplace cares about, such as driving sales, client satisfaction, efficiency, collaboration, etc., you can focus on excelling and gathering proof of your talents in those domains. Make sure what you spend time bettering align with the items that show up on your performance appraisal. This alignment sets you up for the strongest reviews and fastest advancement.

Getting Feedback on Blind Spots

An additional strategy is soliciting candid feedback from others on your skills, work products, and collaboration style. Target trusted colleagues, mentors, or even your manager. Ask them to point out any blind spots where you may be unaware of development needs or performance gaps. Listen with an open mind, resisting any initial defensiveness.

Use their critiques to honestly assess your abilities versus what is expected in roles you want. Look for recurring themes about weaknesses to address or strengths to build upon further. Then act upon this feedback with targeted improvements. You may be oblivious to shortcomings hindering your progression, so others' input offers rare valuable insight.

Self-Evaluating Your Skills

It also helps to personally grade your talents in every area relevant to your job. This allows you to judge where you can still gain mastery.

For each major skill, honestly rate yourself on a scale like: novice, proficient, expert. Gauge both your abilities now and your level when you started in the role. Any major gaps indicate zones to bolster with further practice and education.

Prioritize enhancing skills that are heavily utilized in your position and vital to the quality of your contributions. Focus first on raising proficient areas to expert versus novice to proficient. Deepening your existing strengths has a greater impact than broadening skills from scratch.

Increasing Visibility

Beyond sharpening abilities, also raise your visibility with decision-makers whose opinions influence career advancement. Volunteer for high-profile assignments that provide an opportunity to impress executives. Speak up in meetings with senior leadership present. Join important committees that give exposure to those at the top. Attend social events where mingling allows networking with higher-ups.

Also proactively share your wins and accomplishments with leaders who may not see your day-to-day work. This keeps you relevant in their minds for new openings and promotions. Find natural ways to let them know of your unique value and talents. Just avoid seeming like a braggart.

Becoming the Expert on an Emerging Issue

Developing deep knowledge on an emerging topic important to your company is another avenue for attention and growth. Identify a trend in your industry that will only grow in relevance. Dive into fully understanding it before anyone else does. Position yourself as an expert source your colleagues rely on to explain this issue and predict implications.

Lead the charge in preparing your organization for capitalizing on the opportunity or overcoming the challenge. Share articles, give lunch-and-learns, publish blogs, present to executives - provide value by disseminating your wisdom. When you establish yourself as a pioneer thinker on changes affecting your workplace, people will take notice.

Finding a Mentor

Finally, seek out a more seasoned professional willing to mentor you. Choose someone well-respected who understands your company's unwritten rules of advancement. Meet regularly to hear their objective advice on boosting your skills, overcoming obstacles, and opening doors. Be receptive to tough feedback.

Ask your mentor to make introductions to influential contacts. See if they will recommend you for prized assignments. Request their advocacy when promotion opportunities arise. With the guidance and backing of someone invested in your growth, you gain a invaluable asset for developing your career - even without company support.

Conclusion

While lacking organizational career development programs is far from ideal, you still have options to take your professional future into your own hands. Be proactive with self-assessment, seeking feedback, building expertise, increasing visibility, and finding a mentor. With concerted effort over time, you can create the conditions for your continued success independent of your employer's involvement. It requires perseverance through roadblocks, but the control and empowerment of directing your own advancement is well worth it.

Chapter 16

Crisi-Proofing Your Career in Uncertain Times

The COVID-19 pandemic has demonstrated the importance of adaptability and resilience for organizations and individuals alike. With entire industries disrupted and global economic uncertainty ahead, it's more crucial than ever to take proactive steps to crisis-proof your career. By managing your skills, network, and mindset effectively, you can gain control over your professional trajectory even during periods of massive change.

In this chapter, we will explore how to take charge of your career during crises. First, we will discuss creating and demonstrating value by generously sharing information and ideas when companies need all hands on deck. Next, we will explore the benefits of learning on the job and making internal connections outside your formal role. Finally, we will provide guidance on evaluating whether your role and industry have growth potential, or if you should seek opportunities elsewhere.

With deliberate planning and a flexible mindset, you can future-proof your skills, add value to your organization, and take purposeful action to advance your career, no matter the external circumstances. The insights below will position you to thrive during times of instability and come out stronger on the other side.

Demonstrating Value by Sharing Insights and Ideas

When organizations are in crisis management mode, they need all team members to step up, share expertise, and provide innovative ideas. Rather than retreating or solely focusing on your formal job description, look for ways to create value by providing important industry information, analysis, and recommendations.

For instance, you may have access to research reports, webinars, or newsletters with timely data about how your sector is responding to current challenges. Offer to distribute or present key findings to colleagues who will find them useful. Volunteer to compile competitive intelligence or put together a list of crisis management best practices used in your industry.

This is also the time to develop your own original perspectives and solutions. Do in-depth research on emerging trends and pain points. Come up with strategies for overcoming roadblocks caused by the crisis. Present data, scenarios, and ideas to execs to inform critical decisions. Look for ways your organization can serve customers better or differentiate itself in the current climate.

Stepping forward with vital information, strategic insights, and innovative solutions demonstrates initiative and care for the company. It builds your visibility and value as a thought leader during difficult times. While an "all hands on deck" crisis can be stressful, embracing the opportunity to share your expertise helps the organization while positioning you for future growth.

Making Connections and Learning Across the Organization

In a crisis, silos break down out of necessity. To pivot quickly, companies need collaboration and idea sharing across departments. Be proactive during this time about expanding your skills and making connections across the organization.

Seek out learning opportunities that stretch your capabilities and gain exposure to diverse roles. Ask colleagues in other divisions if you can sit in on virtual meetings, collaborate on projects to support their priorities, or get an overview of how they approach challenges.

Maybe volunteer to spend a few hours a week supporting an overloaded team, offering your helpdesk, writing, or analytical skills. Learn more about how decisions get made from company leaders by asking for mentoring conversations.

Look for chances to build relationships and learn workflows beyond the scope of your normal responsibilities. Developing competencies across functions and building social capital company-wide will enhance your resilience.

When the crisis stabilizes, you'll be able to bring more value through your expanded business acumen. You'll have insight into how the whole organization operates and key relationships across divisions. Investing in cross-training and knowledge sharing now will help you take on increased responsibility later.

Evaluating Industry and Role Growth Potential

The pandemic has turned some industries upside-down, while catalyzing growth for others. Take time to objectively assess whether your role and sector have room for expansion once conditions stabilize. This evaluation can help you determine if you should upscale in your current job or explore new opportunities.

First, analyze your industry's projected growth. Factors to research include technological disruptions, shifts in consumer preferences, restructuring, and new opportunities created by the crisis. If your sector is poised for expansion, identify skills needed to take advantage of those opportunities.

For example, the rise of telemedicine during COVID-19 increased demand for online patient portals and virtual care infrastructure. Healthcare IT specialists with those e-health skills would be well positioned for growth.

Next, consider potential in your specific role. Do projects in your pipeline indicate headcount, responsibility, or budget increases when operations normalize? Have leaders mentioned plans to develop your role? If promotions, raises, or increased scope seem feasible, invest now in skills training to capitalize on that growth.

However, flat team budgets or staffing reductions may signal it's time to look elsewhere. Reflect honestly on whether there's a career path for advancement in your current company and function. If the picture looks murky, spruce up your resume and start networking.

With some industries in flux, being open-minded about new opportunities is key. Focus on transferable skills and keep sight of your long-term goals. With strategic foresight, you can pivot into growth sectors.

Conclusion

The coronavirus pandemic has necessitated agility, resilience, and proactivity in managing our careers. By embracing an "all hands on deck" mindset, making internal connections across the organization, and evaluating our growth potential, we can crisis-proof our professional journeys during uncertain times.

Demonstrating value to your company now by generously sharing information, insights and ideas will build your reputation as a leader. Cross-training and forging relationships beyond your day-to-day role expands your skills. And assessing your industry and position with an eye toward future growth allows you to make deliberate moves rather than reacting passively.

With deliberate planning, resourcefulness and care for your organization, you can take purposeful action to advance your career no matter the external conditions. By following the guidance above, you can future-proof your skills, maximize your adaptability, and come through crisis ready to succeed at higher levels. The insights in this chapter will help you maintain control over your professional trajectory during periods of instability so you can build the career you want, crisis or no crisis.

Chapter 17

The Silver Workforce as Your Competitive Secret: Future-Proofing Your Business for Long-Term Success

In the dynamic landscape of the modern workforce, the proverbial silver lining lies in the aging workforce. A recent global study by Bain & Company forecasts a significant shift, with 150 million jobs transitioning to workers over the age of 55 by 2030. If this transformative trend isn't already part of your strategic planning discussions, it's high time to reconsider. Forward-thinking companies are now championing the business case for embracing, retraining, and supporting older workers—not merely as a choice, but as a strategic necessity.

The prevailing tide of earlier retirements is slowly reversing due to a myriad of factors, including delayed entry of younger individuals into the workforce, a robust job market, inflation, diminishing savings, and a desire among many to extend their contributions beyond traditional retirement ages.

Presently, 25-30% of the U.S. workforce is over 55, and this percentage is on the rise. Surprisingly, most companies have yet to incorporate this demographic shift into their long-term business strategies. Even more disconcerting, many employers view an aging workforce through a lens of increased insurance premiums, potential workers' compensation claims, retraining costs, and other perceived negatives. It's time for a paradigm shift – the advantages of tapping into the wisdom of the aging worker far outweigh any initial financial considerations. As the saying goes, "If you can't get out of it, get into it!"

Wisdom, often described as a blend of experience, knowledge, and intuition, fully matures over time. Intuition, an oft-overlooked skill, emerges from experience and knowledge, making it an invaluable asset. While younger workers form the cornerstone of long-term manpower planning strategies, their development requires significant investment in training and time to accrue experience, knowledge, and intuition.

Enter the older worker—a demographic rich in skills and experience, eager to contribute. They bring an immediate positive impact to productivity, coupled with a strong work ethic and a desire to mentor younger colleagues. This intergenerational collaboration not only strengthens teams but also aligns with a company's diversity, equity, and inclusion (DEI) initiatives. Older workers, by informally mentoring and coaching, play a pivotal role in training the next generation of workers. Numerous studies have highlighted this as a key motivator for older workers choosing to extend their careers.

Strategy, leadership, and culture are interconnected. The positive cultural impact of an aging workforce necessitates a well-thought-out strategy, and the effectiveness of that strategy hinges on leadership. Simon Sinek wisely remarked, "So goes your leaders, so goes your culture. So goes your culture, so goes your company." None of these elements should be taken for granted or expected to develop organically.

How, then, can companies craft a strategy to harness the wisdom of the aging workforce? It begins with acknowledging the aging trend in the U.S. workforce and recognizing it as a strength and unique opportunity rather than a threat. Understanding that the needs of older workers are distinct, ranging from flexible schedules to training in current technologies and customized insurance and retirement plans, is crucial. Additionally, considering the type of work they find meaningful at this stage in their careers becomes vital. Motivated by a sense of purpose, older workers often find fulfillment in mentoring younger colleagues. Effectively managing these opportunities can profoundly impact workplace culture.

As the saying goes, 'culture eats strategy for breakfast,' and this rings true universally in business. Culture, as Simon Sinek reminds us, is only as good as leadership. To fully integrate an aging worker population, leaders must focus on developing competencies to lead a multi-generational workforce, leveraging the unique contributions of older workers.

Culture is a delicate entity. Its development requires intentionality, combining strategy and purpose. The impact of culture on an organization's results directly affects the bottom line. Embracing an older worker population and crafting a strategy to optimize their wisdom is not just a business decision; it's a wise investment in your company's future success.

In conclusion, the growing trend of an ageing worker population presents numerous advantages. However, many employers are aware of this shift but remain inactive. Your culture is your competitive advantage, and the key lies in optimizing the resources of all employees, with special recognition of the unique contributions of the older worker. Make this a crucial component of your strategic planning discussions, as being unprepared for this demographic shift will leave you at a competitive disadvantage.

Chapter 18

Overcoming Self-Doubt: Why You Should Apply for That Job Even if You Don't Meet All the Criteria

When a desirable job posting catches your eye, it can be tempting to immediately click "apply now" in excitement. However, many soon-to-be applicants stop themselves short after thoroughly reading the job description, realizing they do not meet 100% of the required qualifications. This phenomenon is especially prevalent among women in the workforce. According to research, women are 16% less likely than men to apply for a job after viewing the job posting, often because they do not fully meet the listed criteria. Additionally, women on average apply to 20% fewer jobs than men overall. This application gap persists despite the fact that men typically apply to jobs after meeting only 60% of qualifications. So why are women holding themselves back? Imposter syndrome and a lack of confidence are likely major factors. However, much of the initial criteria provided in job postings, especially regarding years of experience for entry-level roles, are negotiable. Rather than counting yourself out, you should view these postings as a starting point for determining your fit. With proper preparation and a compelling application, you just might land your dream job, even if you don't check every box.

Do Your Research

When you come across a job that interests you but you don't quite meet the minimum experience requirements, take some time to research the company and role before deciding whether or not to apply. The initial criteria provided are not necessarily set in stone or absolute requirements. The hiring manager may be flexible regarding certain qualifications depending on the strength of the rest of your application and alignment with the company's needs. Investigate the priorities and needs for the role as well as the company culture. You may find that you can make a compelling case for your candidacy based on skills, perspectives, and experience you do bring to the table. Rather than focusing on what you lack on paper, emphasize the unique value you can contribute if given the chance. Your research will help you tailor your application accordingly.

Craft a Strong, Personalized Cover Letter

While cover letters are optional, they represent a key opportunity to explain why you are an excellent fit despite not meeting the minimum criteria on paper. Your resume will showcase your skills and background, but the cover letter is your chance to provide context, focus on strengths relevant to this specific role, and clearly convey your passion. Use the cover letter to expand on aspects of your candidacy that may not be obvious from your resume alone. Thoroughly describe how your experience, both professional and personal, equips you with the perfect foundation to take on the responsibilities of the role. Provide examples that characterize your work ethic, problem-solving abilities, relationship building skills, or other qualities prioritized in the job description. Keep it targeted and concise, personalized to the company and role. The cover letter is your chance to make a compelling case for why they should take a closer look at your application despite the lack of years of experience.

Use the STAR Method to Demonstrate Your Capabilities

The key to overcoming the experience gap is demonstrating how your existing skills and accomplishments are applicable to the role at hand. This is your opportunity to reassure the employer that although you technically may not meet the minimum criteria, you are capable of excelling in this position. When describing your qualifications and background in your resume, cover letter, and interview, rely on the STAR method. This involves outlining the Situation you faced, the Task you needed to complete, the Action you took, and the Result of your efforts. Select relevant examples that exemplify skills listed in the job description such as project management, relationship building, problem solving, leadership, communication, and other areas of expertise they require. Although your experiences may not have been in the same industry or role, you can draw clear parallels that reinforce your ability to adapt and thrive.

Brush Up on Your Knowledge

In addition to soft skills, most job descriptions list required technical capabilities or industry-specific expertise. Make sure to refresh and strengthen your knowledge in those areas. Spend time learning about the company's products, services, clients, and competitors. Read industry publications and take online courses related to the field. Although you may not have years of direct experience to draw from, you can develop an understanding of the technical skills needed to succeed in the role. Then, reference your knowledge and motivation to continue learning in your application. This will help reassure the employer that you have the foundation to quickly get up to speed.

Conclusion

When an exciting job opportunity catches your eye, muster the courage to apply, even if you do not meet 100% of the required criteria. Do your research to determine areas of potential alignment and value you could bring to the role. Craft a strong, personalized cover letter that frames your experience as an asset, despite the lack of years on your resume. Use the STAR method to compellingly demonstrate how you have built the foundation of knowledge and skills critical for success through past experiences. While you may not look like the ideal candidate on paper, have confidence in your capabilities and potential. With the right preparation and pitch, you just might convince that hiring manager to take a chance on you. Apply strategically and highlight the unique perspective you offer. Don't allow arbitrary experience requirements to limit your potential without even giving it a shot. You are capable of far more than a checklist of criteria can capture on paper.

145

Chapter 19

Unleashing Hidden Potential: Strategies for Identifying and Maximizing Underused Employees

In the dynamic world of business, it's crucial for leaders to identify and tap into the hidden potential of their employees. This chapter delves into strategies for recognizing underused talent within your organization and empowering them to thrive.

By implementing these approaches, you can unlock the full potential of your workforce.

Use the Cross-Functional Approach

Encouraging employees to explore various facets of your organization is a key strategy in workforce development. By fostering a cross-functional approach, employees gain a broad spectrum of skills and insights, enriching their professional experience. This kind of broad exposure is instrumental in uncovering hidden talents and interests, thereby nurturing more engaged and versatile team members. Such a proactive approach not only breaks the monotony of routine tasks but also uncovers potential in unexpected areas of the organization, enhancing overall productivity and innovation.

Foster Collaborations

Create an environment where employees feel comfortable consulting and collaborating with each other. Cross-team interactions can lead to innovative solutions and improved productivity. Encouraging a culture of open communication and teamwork allows underutilized employees to demonstrate their capabilities and ideas. This collaborative atmosphere not only boosts morale but also fosters a sense of belonging and purpose among team members.

Provide More Training and Education

Offering avenues for employees to enhance their skills through further education is a forward-thinking strategy. By supporting them in pursuing specialized degrees, such as in cybersecurity, employees can explore the benefits of this knowledge in protecting their company's digital assets. Online degree programs, in particular, provide the necessary flexibility for employees to effectively balance their work and studies. This investment in their professional development not only yields significant benefits for the organization but also immensely contributes to the personal growth of the employees.

Opportunities for Progression and Promotion

Identify potential leaders within your organization and provide clear pathways for advancement. Promote a culture of meritocracy, where those who excel are rewarded with greater responsibilities and positions. By setting up a transparent system for progression, you encourage employees to strive for excellence and take initiative. This approach ensures that your most promising employees are recognized and given the opportunity to flourish.

Mentoring Programs

Implement mentoring initiatives to connect experienced employees with those eager to learn and grow. This relationship fosters knowledge transfer, guidance, and support, creating a nurturing environment for underused employees to develop their skills and confidence. Mentoring can bridge gaps in experience and understanding, paving the way for a more cohesive and capable workforce.

Regular One-on-One Meetings

Establish a practice of regular, individual meetings between managers and employees. These meetings facilitate open communication, goal setting, and personal development. They provide a platform for employees to express their aspirations, challenges, and feedback. Regular interactions help managers identify underutilized talents and align employee goals with organizational objectives.

The strategic recognition and enhancement of underused employees' potential is vital for every company leader. By engaging these employees in varied aspects of the business, fostering a culture of collaboration, providing opportunities for further education and skill development, etc., leaders can unlock a reservoir of latent talent. Such initiatives not only optimize the workforce but also contribute significantly to the overall success and innovation of the organization. Ultimately, this approach leads to a more dynamic, skilled, and motivated team, driving the company towards greater achievements.

BUILDING HIGH-PERFORMING ORGANIZATIONS

Part 3

Culture and Engagement

Chapter 20

Improving Meeting Conversations Through Permission and Safety

Meetings are an essential part of any organization, allowing teams to align, make decisions, and solve problems together. However, many meetings fall short of their potential, filled with guarded conversations that tiptoe around key issues. How can leaders transform their meetings into open forums for candid discussion and collective insight? The key is to focus on two areas: giving permission and creating safety.

Giving Explicit Permission

One of the simplest yet most powerful things a meeting leader can do is give participants direct and explicit permission to fully express themselves. Permission allows people to seek what they want, give honest feedback, and speak up about problems. Without it, people may hold back out of uncertainty about what's allowed or fear of negative consequences.

Leaders can grant permission through clear invitations, questions, and statements. For example, at the start of a meeting, a leader might say, "I want this to be a space where everyone feels free to share their true perspectives, ask any question on their mind, and have an honest dialogue together." Direct permission-giving statements like this free people to participate more fully.

Leaders can also invite permission-seeking from the group, asking members what permissions would help them contribute fully. This empowers individuals to define what they need to speak and act freely. When leaders actively grant the permissions people request, it builds trust and psychological safety.

Creating Safety

In addition to permission, psychological safety is critical for free-flowing meeting conversations. Safety means people can voice views, ask questions, or admit mistakes without fear of embarrassment or retaliation. Without safety, people censor their words and withhold their true thoughts.

Leaders play a key role in fostering safety by how they respond to contributions in the meeting. Three specific behaviors build safety:

1. Giving full attention to each speaker, actively listening without distraction or interruption. This shows respect and care for each person's perspective.

2. Allowing space for people to take their time expressing thoughts. Resisting the urge to jump in or complete others' sentences provides patience for ideas to emerge.

3. Sharing appreciation for people's questions and comments by identifying what is helpful or insightful about them. This builds trust that all contributions have value.

Beyond leader responses, the overall environment also impacts safety. Having regular members, a relaxed setting, and non-hierarchical participation increase comfort to speak openly. Psychologically safe meetings are grounded in mutual care, respect, and empathy.

The Benefits of Permission and Safety

When leaders consciously cultivate permission and safety in meetings, the benefits are profound. Conversations become more candid, creative, and constructive. People share deeper insights and challenges that they would otherwise keep to themselves. Diverse views get welcomed into the dialogue rather than suppressed. Difficult issues and interpersonal problems can get raised and resolved. Teams leverage their collective wisdom much more effectively.

In psychologically safe meetings, leaders also get more honest feedback and input, gaining invaluable understanding about how their ideas and strategies are being received. And team members feel valued for their perspectives and empowered to do their best work together.

On the other hand, without adequate permission and safety, meetings underperform. Conversations stay superficial, guarded, and sterile. People hold back concerns, reinforce each other's assumptions, and avoid challenging the status quo. Hidden tensions simmer under the surface. Important issues never get addressed. And groupthink limits exploration of alternatives. The organization misses out on innovating and improving.

Permission and safety unlock a group's full potential. They enable the shared vulnerability, candor, and trust that allow meaningful conversations. By being intentional about fostering permission and safety, leaders can dramatically increase the freedom, engagement, and impact of meeting interactions. When people feel free to express their real thoughts and emotions, that's when collaboration truly flourishes.

Conclusion

Creating an environment of permission and safety is foundational to having productive, honest dialogue in meetings. Leaders play an essential role through directly granting permission, inviting the permissions that individuals need, and responding with care and respect to foster safety. With permission and safety established, teams can have more authentic, vulnerable, and courageous conversations, leading to greater collective insight, innovation, and performance. Leaders who aspire to bring out the best in their people must make their meetings a safe space for truth-telling and genuine connection by focusing on permission and safety.

Chapter 21

Toxic Resilience: A Top-Down Issue in the Workplace

In today's fast-paced and competitive work environment, resilience has become a highly valued trait among employees. However, there is a dark side to resilience that can have detrimental effects on employees' mental health and well-being. This phenomenon is known as toxic resilience.

In this chapter, we will explore the concept of toxic resilience, its impact on employees, and the role of management and HR departments in addressing this issue.

What is Toxic Resilience?

Toxic resilience refers to the expectation that employees should be able to handle excessive stress, pressure, and adversity without breaking down or showing signs of weakness. This expectation often stems from management's desire to increase productivity and maintain a competitive edge in the market. As a result, employees are encouraged to push themselves beyond their limits, ignore their mental health, and adopt unhealthy coping mechanisms.

The Impact of Toxic Resilience on Employees

The impact of toxic resilience on employees can be severe and long-lasting. Some of the common effects include:

- Burnout: Employees who are expected to be resilient at all times may experience burnout, which can lead to decreased productivity, absenteeism, and turnover.

- Mental Health Issues: The constant pressure to perform can lead to mental health issues such as anxiety, depression, and post-traumatic stress disorder (PTSD).

- Decreased Morale: When employees feel that their well-being is not being prioritized, they may become disengaged, demotivated, and lose interest in their work.

- Poor Work-Life Balance: Toxic resilience can lead to an unhealthy work-life balance, causing employees to neglect their personal lives, relationships, and self-care.

The Role of Management in Addressing Toxic Resilience

Management plays a crucial role in addressing toxic resilience in the workplace. Here are some ways they can do it:

- *Lead by Example*: Managers who practice toxic resilience themselves can set a harmful example for their employees. Instead, they should prioritize their own mental health and well-being, and demonstrate healthy coping mechanisms.

- *Recognize and Support Employees*: Managers should be able to recognize the signs of burnout and mental health issues in their employees and provide support and resources to help them.

- *Encourage Open Communication*: Management should foster an environment where employees feel comfortable discussing their mental health and well-being without fear of judgment or repercussions.

- *Promote Healthy Coping Mechanisms*: Management can encourage healthy coping mechanisms such as mindfulness, meditation, and exercise, and provide resources for employees to access these services.

The Role of HR Departments in Addressing Toxic Resilience

HR departments also have a vital role in addressing toxic resilience in the workplace. Here are some ways they can do it:

- *Provide Training*: HR departments can provide training for managers and employees on mental health, well-being, and healthy coping mechanisms.

- *Develop Mental Health Policies*: HR departments can develop and implement mental health policies that promote a healthy work environment, provide resources for employees, and address issues related to toxic resilience.

- *Encourage Self-Care*: HR departments can encourage self-care by providing resources such as employee assistance programs (EAPs), mental health days, and flexible work arrangements.

- *Monitor and Address Burnout*: HR departments can monitor employee burnout and address it by providing resources and support, and working with management to make changes to the work environment.

Conclusion

Toxic resilience is a pervasive issue in today's fast-paced and competitive work culture. It can have severe consequences for employees' mental and physical health, job satisfaction, and overall well-being. To address this issue, it's essential for organizations to recognize the signs of toxic resilience and take proactive steps to promote a healthy work environment. This includes fostering open communication, encouraging self-care, and providing resources to support employees' mental health. Additionally, management must lead by example and prioritize their own mental health and well-being. By taking these steps, organizations can create a workplace culture that values and supports employee well-being, rather than perpetuating a culture of toxic resilience. Ultimately, it's up to all of us to break the cycle of toxic resilience and create a healthier, more sustainable work environment for everyone.

Chapter 22

How to Stop Taking Work So Personally

Taking things personally at work is a common issue that many professionals face. While being passionate about your job and feeling a deep sense of responsibility can be positive traits, it's also easy for your work performance to become too intertwined with your self-worth. This can lead to unnecessary stress, anxiety, and even burnout over time.

In this chapter, we will explore how to approach work situations with greater objectivity, clarity and emotional balance.

Learning to separate your self-identity from your professional role is an important skill that allows you to navigate your career with less suffering and more sustainability.

First, we will provide an overview of why people tend to take work so personally and the downsides of this tendency. Next, we will outline five recommended techniques to stop equating your value as a person with your job performance. For each strategy, we will expound on the advice and provide tangible examples of how it can be applied in real work settings.

Implementing even a few of these tactics can help you engage in your professional role with more level-headedness, resilience and proper perspective. With less of your self-esteem on the line in every project or interaction, you will be freed up to accomplish great things and advocate for yourself at work from a grounded place.

Why We Take Things So Personally at Work

There are many reasons why it's common for people to closely associate their self-worth with their careers. For starters, we spend a huge portion of our lives at work. The average American works close to 8 hours per day, 40 hours per week. With that much time immersed in our professional responsibilities, our job becomes ingrained as a core part of our identity.

Additionally, performance reviews, promotions, raises and bonuses provide concrete validation of our skills and capabilities. We yearn for positive feedback from managers and recognition for jobs well done. High performers often tie their sense of achievement closely to exceeding expectations and outperforming peers.

However, this excessive personalization comes at a cost. When every mistake feels like failure and each constructive criticism wounds our ego, it takes a heavy psychological toll. Defensiveness, anxiety, resentment and sadness accumulate when our self-esteem relies too heavily on external measures of success at work.

This chronic stress leads to burnout and emotional exhaustion over time. Meanwhile, companies suffer from lower creativity, innovation and collaboration when employees are mired in constant self-judgment rather than focused on shared organizational goals.

Fortunately, with intention and practice, there are ways to gain more separation between your personal value and your professional endeavors.

How to Stop Taking Work So Personally

1. Adopt a Growth Mindset

The first technique is to cultivate a "growth mindset" about your abilities. People with fixed mindsets believe talents and intelligence cannot be improved -- you either have them or you don't. Conversely, a growth mindset recognizes that even our deeply ingrained traits and capabilities can be developed incrementally over time through effort.

With a fixed mindset, we harshly criticize each failure as a personal shortcoming. With a growth mindset, we are resilient in the face of challenges, viewing them as opportunities for growth. Setbacks become constructive feedback to learn from rather than data points about your self-worth.

For example, let's say you gave an important presentation at work that did not go as well as hoped. Your manager provided feedback that your delivery seemed under-rehearsed and your slides were text-heavy. With a fixed mindset, you would berate yourself: "I'm such a bad public speaker, I'm doomed to fail." With a growth mindset, you tell yourself: "I have room to improve my presentation skills and just need to put in more preparation time."

2. Separate Your Emotions from Your Actions

Another powerful technique is to build the skill of separating your emotions from your actions. Human beings are wired to closely tie feelings to behavior. But this instinct can be overridden with conscious practice.

Start to notice when criticism or failure triggers difficult emotions like anger, anxiety, defensiveness or dejection. Then, make an intentional choice to pause before reacting. Say to yourself "I am feeling x emotion, but I do not need to act from that place." This creates space to choose more constructive responses aligned with your goals.

With our presentation example, when your manager critiques your performance you may initially feel embarrassed and inadequate. By consciously acknowledging "I feel hurt, but I will not lash out defensively," you can instead reply with "Thank you for the feedback, I will focus on improving my public speaking skills for next time." Your emotions are valid, but your reaction remains professional.

3. Reframe Personalization as Commitment

Also consider reframing the tendency to personalize work as a reflection of commitment, passion or investment as opposed to a sense of self-worth. The goal is not to be detached from your job, but to shape personalization into a healthy form.

Ask yourself, "Is my dedication to high performance coming from care and concern versus fear and self-judgment?" For instance, you may desperately want a project to succeed because you know it will help the company and set your team up for future wins. This form of personal investment is positive. However, if you are only worried about looking competent to earn a promotion, your motivation is less productive.

4. Strengthen Your Sense of Self-Worth

Expanding your identity outside of work is also tremendously helpful to gain perspective. Strengthening community ties and nurturing personal passions bolsters your self-confidence from non-work sources.

Make time for hobbies that have nothing to do with your job. Set meaningful goals in other areas like physical fitness, travel or learning a new skill. Cultivate relationships with people who know you in other contexts besides professional. This diversifies your sense of purpose beyond career achievements.

5. Practice Mindfulness

Finally, mindfulness meditation helps separate fleeting emotions from your core identity. By repeatedly bringing your focus to the present moment in a non-judgmental way, you train your mind to observe feelings without attaching excessive meaning to them.

This builds the "observer self" that can watch your perfectionistic inner critic fuel performance anxiety without identifying with its narrative. Mindfulness has been proven to reduce reactivity, lower stress and boost emotional intelligence - all crucial capacities to navigate work with less personalization.

Conclusion

Taking things too personally at work is common, stemming from desires for achievement and external validation. But self-worth that rests too heavily on professional success comes at a detrimental psychological cost over time. Fortunately, strategies like adopting a growth mindset, separating emotions from actions, broadening your identity outside of work, and practicing mindfulness can help.

Implementing even a few of these techniques promises greater clarity, resilience and fulfillment in your career journey. You will be empowered to show up as your best self at work knowing your inner light is not on the line with every project outcome or manager appraisal. While caring deeply about your contributions, you will have the wisdom to let go of self-judgments that do not serve you or your organization. Your industry knowledge, skills and collaborative spirit will be free to shine bright.

175

Chapter 23

Tackling Burnout: Making Workplaces Healthier

Burnout has become an increasingly concerning issue in recent years, with rates rising steadily across various industries and professions. The World Health Organization's decision to formally classify burnout as an "occupational phenomenon" in 2019 brought greater attention to this workplace crisis. No longer viewed solely as a personal struggle, burnout is now rightly seen as a systemic organizational problem requiring systemic solutions.

In this chapter, we will explore how organizations must take responsibility for creating unhealthy working environments that breed burnout in the first place.

Defining and Diagnosing Burnout

Burnout is a condition characterized by emotional exhaustion, cynicism, and feelings of reduced personal accomplishment resulting from chronic workplace stress. Key symptoms include drained mental energy, impaired task performance, lack of engagement, and diminished morale.

For individuals, the personal costs of burnout are massive – linked to serious physical and mental health risks like anxiety, depression, insomnia, high blood pressure, and cardiovascular disease. Organizations also pay a heavy price, with burnout fueling turnover, absenteeism, lower productivity, and poorer service quality.

Clearly diagnosing burnout is the necessary first step. While burnout manifests at an individual level, closer examination reveals its underlying organizational causes. As the original text argued, burnout is not a personal failing but rather the result of dysfunctional workplace dynamics.

Poor Organizational Hygiene

The metaphor of hygiene emphasizes that organizations have a responsibility to proactively maintain a psychologically healthy work environment, just as proper hygiene prevents the spread of disease.

Hallmarks of poor organizational hygiene include unreasonable workloads, job insecurity, lack of autonomy, office politics, conflict with coworkers/managers, unclear job expectations, long hours, unsupportive leadership, and neglect of work-life balance. Even workplaces that appear well-resourced on the surface may have underlying cultural issues that corrode mental health.

When a workplace routinely permits or implicitly encourages such conditions, burnout inevitably results. No amount of yoga, mindfulness apps, or resilience workshops can protect employees from the grinding strain of unhealthy organizational hygiene. While self-care has its place, the onus is on employers to tackle the root causes of burnout.

The Need for Better Data

Data is a powerful tool for diagnosing and addressing burnout. Organizations often rely on vague gut feelings or basic turnover/engagement metrics. But limited data obscures the true drivers of burnout.

Richer, more specific data paints a clearer picture. Useful sources include company records on absenteeism, disability/workers' comp claims, employee assistance program utilization rates, and healthcare costs. Anonymous employee surveys can also measure perceived stress levels, job satisfaction, work-life balance, and observations of organizational culture.

This data helps organizations identify burnout warning signs at a macro level. Data can also be broken down by department, tenure, demographics, etc. to pinpoint which groups are most affected by unhealthy workplace dynamics. The text rightly argues that such granular data is essential for developing targeted burnout interventions.

Smarter Budgeting

Budgets reflect priorities. When organizations under-invest in employees' psychological health and over-invest in short-term productivity, burnout worsens. The text advocates "micro-budgeting" - carefully examining each budget item's impact on wellbeing.

Ways to align budgets with burnout prevention include: providing paid mental health days; rewarding reasonable workloads, not long hours; funding continuing education; creating wellness spaces; subsidizing child/elder care; hiring mental health staff; purchasing ergonomic equipment; and paying living wages that reduce financial stress.

While such budget reallocations require upfront investment, they repay dividends via healthier, happier, and ultimately more productive employees. Wise financial stewardship treats employee wellbeing not as a cost center but as the long-term business asset that it is.

Integrating Wellness and Wellbeing

Finally, standalone wellness programs are insufficient. Yoga classes and stress management seminars make little difference within fundamentally unhealthy organizations. True wellbeing requires integrating support for employees' mental health into everyday operations.

Examples include training managers to recognize burnout warning signs; evaluating workload distribution during hiring; encouraging vacation usage in policy and practice; providing access to counseling; soliciting employee feedback; fostering social connections; creating employee resource groups; and making self-care convenient through onsite amenities.

Such integration allows support to be accessed by those who need it most. It also reinforces that employee wellbeing is central to the organization, not an ancillary activity relegated to the sidelines.

Conclusion

Burnout has reached crisis levels, and workplaces play a major role in creating the conditions for burnout to thrive. But when organizations recognize their responsibility and take action, they can cultivate work environments where every employee is energized and empowered to thrive. This requires moving beyond band-aid personal solutions to enact lasting systemic change.

Genuine burnout prevention means addressing root causes through improved organizational hygiene, better data, smarter budgeting, and integrated wellbeing. When people feel valued, empowered, supported, and mentally healthy at work, burnout fades away. Both employees and organizations will reap the benefits of healthier, more humane workplaces. Tackling burnout may demand upfront effort and investment, but the rewards are well worth it.

183

Chapter 24

Creating a Lasting Change: What It Really Takes to Build New Habits in the Workplace

One of the greatest challenges of leadership is facilitating organizational change and development. While many initiatives begin with enthusiasm, lasting transformation proves far more difficult. What seems like a simple task of adopting a new routine or behavior often fails to stick. However, behavioral research illuminates the true process required for cultivating enduring modifications.

In this chapter, we will explore habit formation and offer practical, industry-specific examples for building new organizational practices.

Habit Formation Begins with Cue and Reward

According to behavioral scientists, habits rely on the association between a cue, routine, and reward (Lally & Gardner, 2013). The cue acts as a trigger prompting an automatic behavior. Upon executing the routine, the individual experiences a sense of reward - whether intrinsic satisfaction or external positive feedback. Over repeated pairings, this cue-routine-reward loop strengthens the habit (Wood & Neal, 2007). For new routines to stick, leaders must thoughtfully design the process to incorporate strong, consistent cues and meaningful rewards.

Develop Cues that are Clear and Consistent

At the outset, cues for a desired routine should be obvious to help associate the behavior. Consider an accounting firm aiming to encourage paperless billing. Leadership makes submitting digital invoices the only option, removes all physical printers, and prominently displays reminders about "Going Green." These tangible changes create a clear prompt for the electronic submission habit. Over time, as the routine establishes, cues can become more subtle. For lasting impact, ensure cues remain consistent rather than intermittent reinforcements which weaken associations (Lally et al., 2010).

Design Routines that are Simple Yet Impactful

For new behaviors to stick, the routine itself needs a low barrier to entry while providing value. Referring to the accounting example, digital billing submission involves only uploading files rather than printing, stuffing envelopes, etc. Its ease minimizes resistance. However, leaders also stress the routine's importance - how going paperless supports environmental and cost goals integral to the firm's mission and image. Finding the right balance of simplicity and meaning encourages lasting adoption (Lally & Gardner, 2013).

Ensure Rewards are Timely, Relevant and Reinforcing

To cement habits through positive feedback, rewards must follow the routine promptly while directly relating to it. In the example, the accounting software could provide an automatic message thanking staff for their paperless submission. Managers acknowledge such contributions during meetings. Celebrating environmental milestones keeps electronically filed invoices feeling rewarding and reinforcing over time (Wood et al., 2005). Properly executed, this cue-routine-reward association cultivates a sustainable new habit.

Overcoming Resistance through Communication

Change often faces pushback, so clear communication remains vital. Returning to the paperless initiative, leadership frames shifting norms as an opportunity rather than demands. Town halls allow answering concerns and celebrating early adopters. Testimonials from peers reinforce benefits like time savings. A Q&A forum maintains two-way dialogue. Consistent, positive messaging navigates resistance and builds buy-in critical for habit formation's longer term (Kotter, 2012).

While establishing new organizational routines requires careful planning and perseverance, behavioral science underscores that habits prove achievable through deliberate cue-routine-reward design. The following section offers further industry examples applying these evidence-backed principles.

Creating Sustainable Practices in Healthcare

In healthcare, championing better patient outcomes and staff well-being demands cultivating healthy habits. Consider a hospital encouraging nurses to take regular meal breaks amid hectic schedules. Cues include visually posted 30-minute timers and leaders verbally prompting breaks. The simple routine involves leaving the floor for the cafeteria.

Rewards involve free, nutritious meals alongside colleague company, temporarily distancing from stressors. Over time, consistent breaks feel more automatic and support both individual wellness and engagement on the job.

For doctors, electronic health records prove integral yet daunting to adopt. The hospital establishes clear prompts through colored desktop backgrounds signaling to "Document Now" during appointments. Templates streamline the routine while colorful summaries highlight its impact - how records support care quality and reimbursements. Auto-populated fields minimize hassle. Monthly recognition of "E-Champions" keeps the electronic habit motivating long-term.

New Norms in Banking through Intentional Onboarding

Like other industries, cultivating desired behaviors from day one proves key for banks. For their Tellers, positive reinforcement proves especially impactful given direct customer interactions. Here, strong onboarding sets the stage, associating routines like making eye contact, smiling and using names as cues prompt friendly service essential to the brand. Roleplays allow practicing the routines until feeling automatic. Immediate feedback from Leaders using props like "Caught You Caring" cards reward those just starting to build the habit. Over time, positive customer responses themselves reinforce the sustainable new norms of exemplary service.

For Loan Officers too, building confidence benefits all stakeholders. Here the cue involves simple prompts on weekly one-on-ones with managers. The routine focuses on open-ended questions encouraging Officers to discuss even minor successes or setbacks. Rewards involve active listening plus specific, supportive feedback. This empathy-building association strengthens habits of vulnerability and help-seeking critical to officer wellness and performance - a true Win-Win for the individual and organization.

Conclusion

Transforming organizational culture demands more than announcements - it requires intentionally shaping new habits through evidence-backed principles. By thoughtfully designing cues, simple yet purposeful routines and immediate, reinforcing rewards, leaders guide lasting behavioral change. While obstacles invariably emerge, clear communication navigates resistance and builds momentum. With diligent, long-term commitment to this process, any industry can establish new norms facilitating optimal operations and outcomes. Habits prove the driver of deep transformation, and their formation, achievable.

191

Chapter 25

The Power of Appreciation: How to Strengthen Workplace Bonds Through Gratitude

Appreciation is a fundamental element of any strong relationship, including those at work. When employees feel valued and appreciated, bonds within teams strengthen, engagement rises, and organizations reap significant benefits. However, many leaders and employees struggle to express sincere appreciation regularly. Utilizing simple, consistent methods to show gratitude at work can transform workplace culture and interpersonal dynamics.

In this chapter, we will explore easy tactics to demonstrate appreciation daily.

Appreciate People's Presence

A simple but powerful way to show appreciation is by acknowledging people's presence. Thanking coworkers for showing up, despite busy lives outside work, demonstrates their value. Consider saying, "I'm glad you're here today," or, "Thanks for being here," as teammates arrive. If someone seems under the weather, say, "I'm grateful you came in despite not feeling well." Noticing who is missing and reaching out conveys care for their well-being. These small gestures reinforce bonds within teams.

For example, when my coworker Anna arrived late to a staff meeting due to a sick child, I said, "Anna, I'm so glad you could make it. I know juggling a sick kiddo and work isn't easy. Thanks for being here." She smiled and seemed relieved her tardiness wasn't an issue. Later, Anna shared how much that acknowledgement meant during a stressful morning.

Appreciate Ideas and Contributions

Honoring colleagues' expertise and input demonstrates appreciation for their role. When employees share suggestions, make it clear you value their perspective through active listening. Maintain eye contact, ask thoughtful follow-up questions, and thank them for their thoughts.

Highlight teammates' contributions in meetings with leadership. For instance, "Sarah recommended an excellent approach to improve our product testing process. Her idea will really strengthen quality control." Follow up with specific praise to the employee like, "Thanks for that terrific recommendation in our meeting, Sarah. Your perspective as an engineer is so valuable."

When we shine a spotlight on people's ideas, it conveys appreciation for their capability and role. I make sure my direct reports know I rely on their expertise by frequently referencing their guidance when leading projects. Regular, sincere praise encourages them to continue bringing innovative ideas.

Appreciate Lives Outside Work

While work provides community and purpose, it should not subsume employees' lives. Families, hobbies, and personal growth matter too. Expressing interest in people's passions beyond work demonstrates appreciation for them as multidimensional individuals.

Start by learning what interests teammates have outside the office. Initiate conversations about favorite sports teams, TV shows, community service activities, or family vacations. Then, reference those interests in casual interactions. Say things like, "How was your son's volleyball playoff game this weekend?" or "You must be excited for the Taylor Swift concert next month!" Thoughtful questions and comments will stick with people.

Also, respect boundaries and discourage excessive overtime. Model healthy habits like leaving on time, taking lunch breaks, and nurturing interests outside work. An overwork culture hurts morale and well-being. Setting realistic expectations and encouraging balance conveys care for the whole person.

Appreciate Needs for Growth

While promotions and training opportunities are traditional aspects of growth, development also comes through daily challenges and learning from others. Employees feel most appreciated when leaders understand their career goals and provide growth opportunities.

Schedule time with direct reports to learn about their professional aspirations. Then look for chances to assign projects utilizing their skillsets and interests. Aim to be a mentor who guides their growth. Says leadership expert John Maxwell,

"A good leader is focused on helping people reach their full potential." Coworker relationships also offer development opportunities. Suggest peer mentoring or job shadowing for employees with common interests.

Finally, view your team's feedback as a gift rather than criticism. Actively request input on strengths and areas for improvement. Applying their suggestions shows appreciation by signaling you value their insights.

Conclusion

Demonstrating sincere appreciation daily requires concerted effort but yields tremendous rewards in workplace relationships and culture. A little gratitude goes a long way. When leaders and employees apply tactics like valuing presence, honoring contributions, caring about lives outside work, and supporting growth, bonds strengthen exponentially. People feel motivated, engaged, and committed to organizations where simple appreciation is the norm. By taking time to be intentionally grateful, we can transform teams and workplaces.

Chapter 26

Gen Z and DEI: A Generation's Commitment to Change

"This is a generational shift in the belief that these values are really important and foundational to their experiences as workers," — Alvin B. Tillery Jr., director of the Center for Diversity and Democracy at Northwestern University.

Every generation brings certain values with them when they enter the workforce. Values they grew up with, shaped by their understanding of the world, and their experiences. The baby boomers grew up with parents who were driven by their experience of hardship through the Great Depression and a world at war, and consequently valued hard work, loyalty, and a sense of optimism deriving from the U.S's success in a post-war world.

Gen X, the children of the hard-working baby boomers, often grew up in a household with two working parents, latchkey kids who had to learn to fend for themselves, while their parents were away. Resourceful and independent, these Gen X entered the workforce at a time when 21st century technology was experiencing its first boom and they understood intimately the advantages therein. Indeed, it's no coincidence that the two most prominent technocrats of our time—Jeff Bezos and Elon Musk—are both from this generation.

Millennials, in some ways, have had it much better than our predecessors. As the most educated generation alive, they represent the majority of the working population today (though not for much longer) and have grown up at a time of unprecedented peace across a majority of the world. Our society is far more diverse and multicultural than ever before, and this generation knows the importance of representation in our workplaces.

But at the same time, millennials are also a generation that has lived through two economic crises, seen the boom, bust, and second coming of IT, witnessed rising debt and inflation, falling wage benefits, environmental anguish, and the all-consuming rise of social media. They strongly value diversity, environmental sustainability, and eco-social awareness yet progress has not always been apparent. Caught between the expectations of the past and the values of the future, millennials are truly a middle generation.

All the while, Gen Z has been watching and learning.

In many ways, Gen Z brings with them the best values of the previous generations. They are fiercely individualistic, yet willing to unite behind a common cause. They've grown up as digital natives, in a world where technology is the premier metric of growth, yet Gen Z is fully aware of the consequences of unsustainability and environmental degradation. They are very value-based in their approach to their work, yet pragmatic, having learnt the futility of rootless idealism from millennials.

Tech-savvy in a way no generation before has been, exposed to online scrutiny from a young age thanks to social media, politically and culturally aware, and purpose driven, Gen Z is not just entering the workforce, they're storming in.

And they have expectations from all of us.

A Highly Connected Generation

Gen Z is the most diverse generation yet. They have grown up in a society that not only appreciates multi-culturalism but takes it for granted. In their schools, colleges, and social circles, most Gen Z Americans have experienced a degree of diversity that is, unfortunately, not reflected in corporate workplaces.

As a generation, they are also highly connected and capable of astonishing organization. As the first generation to be born into a world with social media, they know how to navigate the online space with ease and stay socially and culturally aware. Their unique experiences in a rapidly changing, technologically advanced world have fostered a greater appreciation for diversity and individual identity.

This generation is pushing for changes in labor union issues, social issues, and organizational issues, leading the way in demanding a workplace reset. They expect their employers to rethink what work means to employees today, emphasizing the importance of aligning with their values and priorities

Gen Z Will See Through Corporate BS

"You can say there's no systemic racism, but millennials and Gen Z don't believe that. If you're under 35, you expect these conversations, and if you don't offer them, you'll have trouble recruiting." — Alvin B. Tillery

Jr., director of the Center for Diversity and Democracy at Northwestern University.

Gen Z's significant cultural and political impact is evident in their engagement with issues like climate change, gun control, and social justice. They are redefining social norms, workplace dynamics, and political landscapes with their values-based, pragmatic approach.

What's more, they are fully aware of how paper-thin corporate social responsibility can be and spot a smoke-and-mirrors act from a mile away. Their keen awareness is informed by experiences and observations in the workplace. A Tallo study revealed that 67% of Gen Z respondents had witnessed workplace discrimination and 44% experienced it themselves. This suggests that Gen Z is attuned to the gap between proclaimed diversity policies and actual practices. As VP of Netflix's Inclusion Strategy Verna Myers puts it, *""Diversity is being invited to the party; inclusion is being asked to dance."*

There is a Lot that Can Be Done but Where Do You Begin?

"The modern corporation has evolved to treat workplace discrimination not as an urgent moral or business imperative, but as a manageable PR investment." — Lily Zheng, author and DEI expert

Inculcating diversity is not the same as implementing a new tool, something that can be tacked on to an existing institutional framework. It needs to be inculcated through active goal setting and embedded into the organizational agenda. It needs to be driven by the conscious desire to create a positive change.

Promote diverse leadership

Representation, at all levels of the organization, is crucial for any DEI initiative to succeed. Gen Z needs to see leaders who look like them.

This is not just about racial and ethnic diversity, but also includes gender, sexual orientation, and different backgrounds. The presence of diverse leaders can inspire and empower younger employees, fostering a sense of belonging and inclusion.

A recent study by recruitment portal, Monster.com, found that 83% of Gen Z employees consider a commitment to diversity and inclusion significant when deciding where to work. This expectation for diversity in leadership has only been heightened by the recent reversals in affirmative action at institutions of higher learning.

Top down and bottom up

Author and DEI expert Lily Zheng advocates for a comprehensive approach to diversity that involves both leadership initiative and active employee engagement and feedback. What she calls the *top-down and bottom-up approach.*

Zheng emphasizes the importance of measuring the impact of any policy, process, or practice, particularly from a DEI perspective. Leaders need to overcome their fear of finding potential inequities and audit legacy policies and processes for discrimination. This means admitting ignorance about the experiences of all employees and seeking to understand and correct biases.

Lily Zheng's approach necessitates a thorough examination of existing policies, a commitment from leadership to understanding diverse employee experiences, and a willingness to address and correct institutional biases.

Organizations need to actively seek and value employee feedback, ensuring their concerns and experiences shape policy revisions and implementations.

Learn from outside partners

It's important to remember that with any diversity initiative, there's no need to re-invent the wheel. We have a huge amounts of data to work with and recognize what works.

As a C-suite leader at Peterson Technology Partners, I am privileged to be a part Chief, a professional network of high-level women executives from across the globe. This network has given me the opportunity to connect with brilliant women leaders from various backgrounds and learn from them.

One thing I have learned from this experience is that businesses don't have to build a DEI platform from the ground up. Instead, they can partner with organizations that specialize in customizing DEI initiatives to suit their unique needs. These external organizations can not only be a source of learning for leaders but can also help them audit their existing frameworks to identify problem areas.

Conclusion

Gen Z's entrance into the workforce heralds a new era of values-driven, inclusive, and transparent work culture. Their demand for representation at all levels, particularly in leadership, reflects a broader societal shift towards valuing diversity and inclusivity.

Organizations must adapt by embedding these values into their core operations, actively seeking and valuing employee feedback, and ensuring that policies and practices genuinely reflect these ideals. The future of the workplace depends on our ability to embrace and nurture the diverse perspectives and experiences of Gen Z, creating an environment where everyone, regardless of background or identity, feels valued, respected, and empowered.

As we navigate this shift, the onus is on leaders to foster a culture that resonates with the aspirational and pragmatic ethos of this generation.

Chapter 27

Engaging a Multigenerational Workforce: Best Practices for Unleashing Potential

The composition of today's workforce is changing dramatically. Improved health and longevity mean people are living and working longer, leading to an unprecedented situation where workplaces may contain four or five generations of employees. Each generation brings its own perspectives, values, and priorities. With such diversity comes great potential, but also challenges in engaging and integrating all employees. Successfully fostering an age-inclusive culture is key for organizations that wish to attract and retain top talent across generations, spur innovation, and remain competitive.

In this chapter, we will explore several best practices for effectively engaging the multigenerational workforce.

Fostering Intergenerational Contact and Collaboration

Studies show intergenerational contact and collaboration in the workplace can yield numerous benefits. It builds understanding between age groups, reduces stereotypes, and enables sharing of knowledge and skills. Organizations should provide opportunities for intergenerational teamwork through strategically designed training programs, mentoring initiatives, workgroups, task forces, and community outreach projects.

For example, Cisco implemented a "Shadow Board" program where Millennial employees are paired with and mentored by senior leaders. Participants report gaining insight into leadership styles, organizational history and strategy while relationships strengthened between generations.

Home Depot fosters intergenerational teams by assigning "Youth Captains" to train older workers on using technology. Older employees share institutional knowledge and expertise with younger team members. This enhances collaboration, leverages the strengths of all generations, and ensures knowledge transfer.

customized training that met needs of employees at different career stages. Mid-career employees could take leadership development courses while newer hires received onboarding sessions. Older workers interested in mentoring were offered train-the-trainer programs. The tailored training promoted professional growth for all generations.

Emphasizing Health and Work-Life Balance

Each generation has different health and work-life needs. Best-practice employers recognize this and implement policies that demonstrate care and understanding.

For young parents, onsite daycare, flexible scheduling, and generous family leave signal a family-friendly culture. Businesses that provide dry cleaning, meal services, and concierge benefits make it easier for busy mid-career employees to manage personal and professional demands. Meanwhile, older employees appreciate wellness incentives, reduced travel, flexible hours, and remote work options.

Deloitte actively assesses the needs of its multigenerational workforce through surveys and feedback. Insights gained led to additions like onsite health clinics providing flu shots and physical therapy, deploying ergonomic assessments and equipment, unlimited vacation time, and remote work. The result is a culture supporting employee well-being and work-life fit across all age groups.

Adapting Recruitment and Retention Approaches

Attracting and retaining top talent across generations requires tailored recruiting and retention strategies. Employers should understand what motivates each generation and develop targeted outreach.

Millennials and Gen Z may be swayed by progressive policies around remote work, social consciousness, diversity, equity and inclusion. Gen Xers often look for flexible schedules, career development, work-life balance. Baby Boomers tend to prioritize supportive leadership, meaningful contributions, and flexibility to transition into retirement.

Strategic retention efforts also matter. Prudential Financial increased its under-35 workforce by 29% in two years through initiatives like a mentoring program, leadership academy, and targeted college recruitment. Meanwhile, to retain its 50+ workers, CVS Health developed roles that let retirees stay engaged as consultants or employees on custom schedules. Adapting practices to meet generational needs boosts engagement and talent retention across age groups.

Promoting Cross-Generational Mentoring

Cross-generational mentoring delivers advantages for mentees, mentors, and organizations. Younger mentees can gain insight from experienced mentors who provide valuable coaching, networking contacts, and organizational perspective. For mentors, sharing knowledge solidifies learning and cultivates leadership skills.

At Abbott Laboratories' formal initiative, 95% of mentees and 92% of mentors said participation enhanced their skills and network. Mentoring boosts productivity and job satisfaction while enhancing transfer of institutional knowledge before older workers' departure. Cross-generational mentoring also facilitates relationship-building between diverse employees.

Organizations should incorporate mentorship opportunities as a development tool and culture enhancer. Formal programs with training resources, structured activities, and management support increase success. Company-provided venues and team-building events also help connections flourish. Cross-generational mentoring empower individuals and strengthens organizational culture.

Conclusion

Today's multigenerational workforce offers amazing potential. But realizing the promise requires understanding employees' diverse needs and implementing best practices to support all generations. Encouraging intergenerational contact, emphasizing work-life balance, adapting recruiting and retention, and facilitating mentoring across age groups are proven strategies. With the right approach, employers can create an age-inclusive culture that engages the entire workforce, fosters innovation and productivity, and gives them a competitive edge. Unleashing the potential of the multigenerational workforce is an opportunity forward-thinking organizations cannot afford to miss.

215

Chapter 28

Combating a Culture of False Urgency at Work

In today's fast-paced work environment, it can feel like there is never enough time to complete tasks. Constant connectivity from smartphones and other devices reinforces the idea that work should always be a top priority. However, this "culture of constant connectivity" and never-ending urgency is taking its toll on organizations and employees. While some level of urgency is necessary to meet deadlines and tackle problems, much of the urgency felt on a day-to-day basis is actually false. This false sense of urgency creates unnecessary stress, reduces productivity, and harms employee well-being and retention. As leaders, it is important to recognize the signs of a culture of false urgency and take steps to combat it. By setting clearer boundaries, prioritizing effectively, and focusing on outcomes over activity, leaders can create a more sustainable work environment where employees are engaged and able to do their best work.

In this chapter, we will explore how leadership can combat a culture of false urgency through setting boundaries, prioritizing work effectively, and focusing on outcomes over perpetual activity.

Research Foundations

Scholarly research has demonstrated the negative effects of constant connectivity and a culture of false urgency. Studies have shown that the inability to disconnect from work leads to increased stress, multitasking ineffectiveness, and reduced focus and problem-solving abilities (Mark, Voida, & Cardello, 2012; Mark, Gudith, & Klocke, 2008). When employees feel they must be constantly reactive to emails, messages and minor issues, it reduces strategic thinking and focus on important priorities (Galluch, Grover, & Thatcher, 2015). Leaders play a key role in setting boundaries and culture, so addressing issues of false urgency is important for organizational performance and employee well-being.

Setting Boundaries to Combat Constant Connectivity

One of the key drivers of false urgency in organizations is the inability to disconnect from work due to constant connectivity. Employees feel pressure to constantly monitor and immediately respond to emails, messages and notifications, even when not technically "on the clock." This translates to long work hours and an inability to truly detach from the job. To combat this, leaders must explicitly set boundaries around work hours and expectations of availability.

Research shows that enacting clear work-life boundaries reduces stress, increases engagement, and fosters innovation (Clark, 2000; Kossek et al., 2006). When employees feel pressure to constantly be available, it reduces psychological detachment from work during non-work hours (Sandelands & Buckner, 1989).

Setting Boundaries in Technology: In the technology industry, around-the-clock availability is often the norm due to global operations and quick product release cycles. However, companies like Microsoft have recognized the need to shift this culture. Microsoft issued a "right to disconnect" policy encouraging employees to ignore emails after typical work hours, allowing for recharging (Gibbs, 2014). Google also utilizes an "out-of-office" notifier on emails during non-work hours to signal when a reply may be delayed (Austin, 2018).

Setting clear communication norms like this reduces the pressure to constantly respond.

Setting Boundaries in Consulting: In consulting, travel and long client site schedules may blur work-life boundaries. Firms must communicate clear expectations for non-billable personal time, even on client premises or trips. For example, large consulting firms like Accenture, Deloitte, and PwC prohibit internal emails after typical work hours and strongly discourage client communication during personal evenings and weekends except for important issues. Leaders at these firms coach consultants on utilizing out-of-office messages and ignoring non-urgent requests when officially off-duty.

Setting Boundaries in Healthcare: While 24/7 patient care requires some flexibility, healthcare leaders can still foster boundaries. Hospitals like the Mayo Clinic explicitly state personal time expectations for roles like nurses and physicians to prevent constant work availability. Having on-call coverage and limiting non-urgent notifications after hours to designated staff reduces burnout risks. Outlining clear communication protocols with these parameters sets the tone that personal time away from work is acceptable and prioritized by leadership.

To combat constant connectivity and an always-on culture, leaders across industries must proactively define and role model clear boundaries around work hours and availability expectations. Using email auto-replies, clarifying non-urgent communication blackout periods, and limiting non-work hour notifications reduces the driver of false urgency around perpetual responsiveness.

Prioritizing Effectively to Focus on What Really Matters

When employees feel overwhelmed by the amount of competing priorities and urgent but unimportant tasks, it fosters an environment of false urgency. Leaders play a key role in setting priorities to focus teams on strategic goals and value-adding work.

Studies show ineffective prioritization reduces satisfaction and commitment while increasing stress and turnover intentions (Boyar et al., 2016; Franco-Santos et al., 2014). When employees feel overwhelmed or uncertain about where to focus their efforts, it breeds unnecessary urgency around low-impact tasks.

Prioritization in Technology: At Apple, executives are strict about limiting the total number of company-wide priorities at once to prevent employees from feeling pulled in too many directions (Isaacson, 2011). Management ensures teams focus first on initiatives that directly support key goals, like next product launches or growth strategies. Lower-impact operational tasks only receive attention as bandwidth allows.

Prioritization in Consulting: McKinsey and Bain clarify project prioritization for consultants upfront to ensure strategic client work receives necessary resources and attention. Status reports track progress on the highest impact deliverables first before chasing lower priorities or scope creep. If additional minor tasks arise, leadership assesses importance versus disruptions to current strategic work.

Prioritization in Healthcare: At Johns Hopkins Hospital, leaders utilize priority matrices in staff meetings to ensure clinical and operational teams focus on initiatives directly improving patient outcomes and experience over administrative paperwork or metrics. Projects receive adjusted deadlines or resources if leadership deems them lower impact to current strategic priorities.

In all industries, clearly communicating top priorities and deprioritizing or delaying lower impact work prevents falsely urgent, perpetual reactive behavior. Using prioritization tools at planning and review stages focuses employee efforts on initiatives that move organizational strategy forward.

Focusing on Outcomes Over Endless Activity

When employees feel rushed to constantly be doing something or perceived as busy, it fosters feelings of false urgency. Combating this takes leadership focus on outcomes rather than activity levels.

While activity can boost short-term productivity, excessive focus on staying busy without strategic goals reduces problem-solving, creativity and long-term performance (Amabile & Kramer, 2011). Outcome-focused cultures see 30-50% higher productivity according to multiple studies (Neumann, 2018; Vogus & Singer, 2016).

Outcome Focus at Amazon: Amazon rates professionals not on face time or meetings, but results like new customer acquisition or revenue growth. Employees are empowered to work asynchronously as needed to achieve goals rather endless activity reports (Stone, 2013). This prevents false urgency around busywork over impactful work.

Outcome Focus at Apple: Rather than micro-manage teams, Apple leaders clearly define project objectives and provide autonomy to achieve them however teams see fit (Isaacson, 2011). Progress updates focus on sharing results and addressing roadblocks rather than activity levels or hours worked.

Outcome Focus in Healthcare: At Kaiser Permanente, leaders hold managers accountable for continuously improving key outcomes like health indicators, patient satisfaction and cost of care rather than process adherence or activity metrics (Birney et al., 2016). Teams innovate care delivery as needed to boost outcomes versus forcing activity for activity's sake.

Across functions, clarifying strategic results expected rather than activity behaviors prevents falsely urgent, perpetual busyness that reduces impact. Providing autonomy within clear outcome frameworks shifts focus to quality work over quantity metrics. Regular progress reviews emphasize sharing what was achieved versus listing busy tasks.

Conclusion

In today's hyperconnected workplace, constant connectivity and an endless list of competing priorities fosters a culture of false urgency that reduces employee focus, productivity and well-being. Leaders play a key role in combating this by proactively setting boundaries around work hours and availability, prioritizing teams' efforts strategically, and focusing accountability on outcomes achieved rather than perpetual activity. Whether in technology, consulting, healthcare or other industries, emphasizing quality over quantity of work through clarifying expectations, communicating priorities and reviewing results rather than activities creates a more sustainable work culture. By recognizing and addressing signs of false urgency, organizations see increased employee engagement, retention of top talent and overall performance to better serve customers in today's competitive market.

225

Chapter 29

Building a Culture of Feedback: A Guide to Nurturing Your Team's Most Helpful Ally

In today's fast-paced business environment, it's no secret that feedback is essential for personal and professional growth. However, simply providing feedback is not enough; it's crucial to create a culture where feedback is embraced, valued, and acted upon.

In this chapter, we will explore the mindsets and practices required to build a culture of feedback, where your team can leverage feedback as their most helpful ally.

Embrace a Growth Mindset

The foundation of a culture of feedback is a growth mindset. This means that individuals within the organization believe that their abilities and intelligence can be developed through dedication and hard work. In a growth mindset culture, feedback is seen as an opportunity for growth, rather than a criticism or judgment.

At Google, employees are encouraged to embrace a growth mindset. They believe that everyone has the capacity to learn and grow, and that failure is an opportunity for growth. This mindset is reinforced through regular feedback sessions, where employees are encouraged to share their thoughts and ideas, and receive feedback from their peers and managers.

Create a Safe Space for Feedback

A culture of feedback requires a safe space where individuals feel comfortable sharing their thoughts and receiving feedback. This means creating an environment where everyone feels valued, respected, and free from judgment.

At Zappos, they understand the importance of creating a safe space for feedback. They have implemented a system called "Zappos University," where employees are encouraged to share their feedback and ideas, and receive feedback from their peers and managers. This system has helped create a culture where feedback is embraced and valued, leading to increased collaboration and innovation.

Provide Regular Feedback

Regular feedback is essential for personal and professional growth. It helps individuals understand their strengths and weaknesses, identify areas for improvement, and develop strategies for growth. In a culture of feedback, regular feedback is a norm, and individuals are encouraged to seek and provide feedback frequently.

At Microsoft, they believe that regular feedback is essential for growth and development. They have implemented a system called "MyAnalytics," which provides real-time feedback to employees on their performance. This system helps employees identify areas where they need to improve and provides them with the necessary tools and resources to do so.

Act on Feedback

Providing feedback is not enough; it's essential to act on it. A culture of feedback requires individuals to take action on the feedback they receive, whether it's positive or negative. This means that individuals need to be open to change, willing to learn, and committed to growth.

At Amazon, they understand the importance of acting on feedback. They have implemented a system called "Customer Obsession," which encourages employees to act on customer feedback. This system has helped Amazon become one of the world's most customer-centric companies, with a focus on continuous improvement and innovation.

Celebrate Successes and Failures

In a culture of feedback, successes and failures are both celebrated. This helps to reinforce the growth mindset and encourages individuals to take risks, experiment, and learn from their mistakes.

At Facebook, they celebrate both successes and failures. They believe that failures are an opportunity for growth and learning, and that successes should be celebrated and shared with the entire organization. This culture has helped Facebook become one of the most innovative companies in the world, with a focus on continuous improvement and disruption.

Conclusion

Building a culture of feedback is a crucial step in creating a high-performing team. By embracing a growth mindset, creating a safe space for feedback, providing regular feedback, acting on feedback, and celebrating successes and failures, teams can cultivate a culture that values continuous learning and improvement. This not only helps individuals grow and develop their skills, but also fosters a collaborative and innovative environment that drives business success. By implementing these strategies, organizations can create a feedback-rich culture that helps them stay ahead of the competition and achieve their goals.

Chapter 30

Fostering Mentally Healthy Workplace Culture: Safety, Community, and Organizational Support

The COVID-19 pandemic has dramatically impacted mental health in workplaces across the United States. With heightened stress, anxiety, isolation, and burnout, employees have struggled with declining mental wellbeing over the past few years. However, despite these challenges, new research reveals some bright spots regarding mental health at work. Employees today demonstrate greater awareness and openness about mental health. They increasingly expect and demand more robust mental health support from their employers. What do workers need to thrive mentally on the job today? As a new study by Salvatore et al. explores, employees primarily want what research has always shown works best: mentally healthy workplace cultures centered around psychological safety, community, and organizational support.

In this chapter, we will explore Salvatore et al.'s research, which provides powerful insights into how mental health at work has evolved before, during, and after the pandemic. We will look at the study's key findings regarding employees' perspectives and experiences with mental health, stigma, and work over this tumultuous period. Most importantly, the study details the specific strategies leaders and organizations can implement to foster more sustainable, mentally healthy cultures. This includes promoting: psychological safety and trust; a sense of community and belonging; mental health awareness and education; comprehensive benefits and services; and an organizational commitment to mental wellbeing across policies, programs, and practices.

The Pandemic's Impact on Mental Health at Work

The COVID-19 pandemic dealt an unprecedented blow to mental health across all domains of life, including the workplace. By spring of 2022, rates of depression and anxiety worldwide had increased by 25%, while stress-related disorders surged. This mental health crisis has profoundly impacted employees. Even prior to COVID-19, mental health conditions were the leading cause of disability and lost productivity at work. However, the radical upheaval of the pandemic accelerated concerning trends.

Salvatore et al.'s research examined how the seismic changes of the pandemic affected mental health from the perspective of employees themselves. They conducted a survey of over 1,500 U.S. workers both before COVID-19 and two years into the pandemic. Their findings reveal a complex picture of both progress and persistent struggles when it comes to mental health at work today.

On the one hand, the pandemic appears to have made mental health a more prominent and accepted topic of discussion in the workplace. The percentage of employees who said no one at their company ever discussed mental health fell from 51% pre-pandemic to just 28% in 2022. Additionally, stigma seems to be slowly decreasing, with more workers saying they feel comfortable discussing mental health issues with managers and colleagues.

However, despite this increased awareness and openness, employees' actual mental wellbeing has not improved. Rates of depression, anxiety, loneliness, and burnout all increased substantially during the pandemic and remain elevated today. Employees report higher stress, more challenges concentrating, and reduced ability to manage emotions. Critically, they feel their workplaces have not done enough to address these mounting mental health burdens. 50% say their company culture does not support mental health, while just 22% feel their employers provide sufficient mental health services and benefits.

This mismatch between employees desiring more support and workplaces failing to deliver reveals the need for organizations to move beyond superficial solutions. While initiatives like offering meditation apps or appointing a "Chief Feelings Officer" may generate press, they do little to foster sustainable cultural change. Employees today want meaningful strategies grounded in psychological safety, trust, community, and humane organizational values. The following sections detail specific, research-backed approaches leaders can implement to promote genuine, long-term mental health improvement across their organizations.

Fostering Psychologically Safe Cultures

The foundation of any mentally healthy workplace is psychological safety. Employees need to feel able to express vulnerability, ask questions, and take risks without fear of embarrassment, retaliation, or punishment. Psychological safety establishes a bedrock of trust, enabling authentic communication about mental health without stigma.

Leaders play a pivotal role in cultivating psychologically safe cultures from the top-down. They must model openness and vulnerability by sharing their own mental health experiences and struggles. Leaders should also proactively invite perspectives from employees across levels of seniority and privilege. Structurally, they can implement employee assistance programs that guarantee anonymity and remove barriers to accessing mental health support. Psychologically safe workplaces also have clear, consistently enforced anti-bullying and anti-harassment policies.

Additionally, teams and colleagues create psychological safety through mutual empathy, compassion, and non-judgment. Simple practices like active listening, validating others' emotions, and extending grace all help colleagues feel comfortable discussing mental health. Ultimately, psychological safety enables the honest, judgment-free conversations that allow mental health struggles to be addressed early before escalating into crises.

Building Inclusive Community

Alongside psychological safety, employees strongly desire a sense of community, belonging, and mattering at work. Humans are inherently social; we thrive when we feel connected to those around us. During COVID-19's isolation, many workers lacked these essential social bonds and experienced intensified mental health strains.

Rebuilding community requires thoughtful intention across company culture, policies, and practices. Leaders should foster personal connections and trust by hosting small-group lunches, coffee meetups, and low-pressure social events. Diversity, equity, and inclusion initiatives help ensure all employees feel welcomed and valued for their unique identities and experiences.

During times of distress, coworkers become critical sources of social support. Leaders can empower employees to support colleagues' mental health through mental health ally/advocacy training. This teaches employees how to sensitively yet directly discuss mental health, provide non-judgmental listening, and connect coworkers with resources.

Structurally, buddy systems, mentorship programs, and employee resource groups give employees forums to build community and discuss mental health. Flexible work policies enable employees to maintain crucial social connections outside of work. By proactively strengthening interpersonal bonds and support, organizations cultivate a culture where employees feel less alone in their mental health journeys.

Educating to Reduce Stigma

While stigma around mental health is decreasing, it remains a significant barrier to employees seeking support. Over a third of workers still feel discussing a mental health issue with a manager would be inappropriate. Stigma often stems from lack of awareness and understanding. Thus, continual mental health education can help normalize these issues and empower employees to take action.

Workplaces should provide regular training on mental health literacy, stigma reduction, and suicide prevention. Programs can be integrated into onboarding, leadership development, DEI initiatives, and health/wellness benefits education. Beyond one-off sessions, ongoing learning opportunities through lunch-and-learns, newsletters, and intranet portals reinforce an organizational commitment to mental health.

Training helps employees recognize signs of distress in themselves and others. It teaches them how to compassionately yet directly discuss concerns, while instilling that mental illness should receive the same care and urgency as physical illness. Education also equips managers to identify troubling changes in employees and sensitively broach conversations. When workplaces promote compassionate understanding of mental health, stigma fades.

Access to Comprehensive Mental Health Benefits

Of course, education alone is insufficient without accessible treatment resources. Employees today expect robust mental health benefits that meet their diverse needs. Quality employee assistance programs providing free, confidential mental health counselling are foundational. Workplaces can also partner with digital platforms offering virtual therapy, self-help tools, and convenient access to psychiatric care.

Crucially, mental health benefits should integrate seamlessly with medical coverage. Full parity between physical and mental healthcare reduces cost barriers. Other supportive financial investments include training mental health first aiders and peer counselors. Generous mental sick day allowances enable employees to prioritize recovery.

Benefits only succeed if employees know about and can easily use them. Thus, workplaces must promote offerings through multi-channel outreach while minimizing logistical hurdles. Protecting employees' medical privacy remains paramount. When workplaces make comprehensive, integrated mental healthcare readily available, employees gain essential support.

Embedding Mental Wellbeing in Organizational Values and Systems

Ultimately, standalone policies fail unless undergirded by a culture that values human welfare. Fostering mental health requires embedding wellbeing into an organization's deepest values and structures.

This begins with leaders unequivocally declaring mental health a top priority across strategy, vision, and operations. Dedicated mental health professionals in HR and a Chief Wellness Officer seat mental health concerns firmly in the C-suite. Mental health metrics become integrated into business dashboards, goals, and success indicators.

Work processes and performance management emphasize sustainability, work-life balance, and compassion. Meetings, emails, and Slack adopt norms that do not demand 24/7 availability. Workloads and schedules allow for self-care and renewal. Coaching and development conversations incorporate mental health check-ins.

Mentally healthy cultures also guarantee all employees basic dignity, respect, and mattering. Living wages, paid leave, mental healthcare, and childcare show workers they are valued as full human beings. Anti-harassment and anti-discrimination policies are strictly enforced, with clear, safe reporting processes. When organizations center human welfare across all operations, employees gain the support they need to thrive mentally.

Conclusion

The study on the future of mental health at work highlights the need for safety, community, and a healthy organizational culture. While the findings show that mental health isn't improving overall in the U.S., there are encouraging signs of greater awareness and a shift in focus towards mentally healthier cultures. Employees are looking beyond traditional benefits and technologies, recognizing that what they truly need is a supportive and nurturing work environment. To foster sustainable mental health cultures, leaders must prioritize the well-being of their employees and implement strategies such as promoting open communication, providing resources and support, and creating a culture that values mental health. By prioritizing these aspects, organizations can create a positive and inclusive workplace where employees feel safe, supported, and empowered to thrive both personally and professionally.

243

245

Chapter 31

The Myth of "Caught Up" at Work: Why You Should Stop Feeling Guilty and Embrace Self-Compassion

Do you have a never-ending to-do list at work? Are you constantly feeling guilty or ashamed about the tasks that linger unfinished? You're not alone. Many people struggle with the pressure to constantly produce and feel like they're never "caught up" at work. But what if I told you that feeling guilty or ashamed about it is not only unhelpful, but also harmful to your productivity?

In this chapter, we will explore the difference between guilt and shame, why they're not useful emotions in the workplace, and how you can practice self-compassion and acceptance to achieve a healthier work-life balance.

The Psychology of Guilt and Shame at Work

Guilt and shame are often used interchangeably, but they're actually distinct emotions.

Shame is Rarely Helpful

Feeling ashamed about unfinished work stems from a sense that one has failed or is somehow fundamentally flawed or incompetent. However, research shows shame is an unproductive emotion that harms motivation and focus. When people feel ashamed, they are more likely to withdraw, procrastinate, or engage in self-blame rather than take meaningful action. Shame triggers the body's "fight or flight" stress response, flooding us with cortisol that impairs cognitive functioning. To minimize shame's negative impact, it is important not to define one's self-worth by productivity levels or attach too much personal value to specific tasks left undone.

Guilt Can Motivate but Also backfire

Unlike shame, feelings of guilt can potentially motivate someone to finish an overdue task. However, excessive or prolonged guilt often does more harm than good. Mild, short-term guilt may light a fire to wrap up an important project. But chronic guilt wears us down over time and reduces efficacy by eating away at mental and emotional reserves. When guilt spirals into rumination about all we haven't finished instead of focusing on solutions, it paralyzes progress. Guilt also loses its utility outside of work, as evenings and weekends should be for rest and recharging instead of constantly rehashing workload stresses.

The Illusion of Ever Being "Caught Up"

No matter how efficiently one works, it is unrealistic and unnecessary to expect to constantly stay on top of every task. Workloads ebb and flow, and periods of being slightly behind are normal and even necessary for productivity in the long run. Trying to maintain an impossible standard of always being fully "caught up" sets oneself up for chronic guilt, burnout, and diminishing returns. Accepting that some tasks will inevitably remain incomplete at any given time is a healthier perspective that prevents wasteful rumination over normal workload fluctuations.

Why Guilt and Shame Are Unhelpful at Work

Guilt and shame are not only unhelpful at work, but they can also be harmful to your productivity and well-being. Here are a few reasons why:

- *They create a negative work environment*: When you're constantly feeling guilty or ashamed, it can create a toxic work environment. You may become irritable, snappish, or withdrawn, which can affect your colleagues and team morale.

- *They lead to burnout*: Constantly striving to be "caught up" can lead to burnout. When you're feeling guilty or ashamed, you may work longer hours, skip breaks, or take on too much, which can lead to exhaustion and decreased productivity.

- *They distract you from the task at hand*: When you're consumed by guilt or shame, it's difficult to focus on the task at hand. You may find yourself ruminating on what you haven't done instead of concentrating on what you need to do.

- *They undermine self-confidence*: Guilt and shame can make you feel like you're not good enough or capable enough. This can lead to self-doubt and a lack of confidence, which can hinder your ability to complete tasks efficiently.

Practicing Self-Compassion and Acceptance

So, if guilt and shame are unhelpful at work, what can you do instead? Here are a few strategies to help you practice self-compassion and acceptance:

- *Exercise self-compassion*: Treat yourself with kindness, understanding, and patience. Remember that everyone makes mistakes and it's okay to not be perfect.

- *Focus on what you have achieved*: Instead of dwelling on what you haven't done, focus on what you have achieved. Celebrate your successes, no matter how small they may seem.

- *Practice acceptance*: Accept that you're not going to be "caught up" at work all the time. It's okay to have a never-ending to-do list. Instead of fighting it, embrace it and focus on what you can do in the present moment.

- *Embrace Imperfect Action*: Take action on tasks even if you don't have all the information or resources. Imperfect action is better than no action at all.

- *Set Realistic Goals*: Set realistic goals that align with your priorities and values. Break down big tasks into smaller, manageable chunks, and focus on one task at a time.

Conclusion

Feeling guilty or ashamed about not being "caught up" at work is a common experience, but it's not a productive or healthy one. Instead of beating ourselves up over what we haven't done, we should focus on what we have achieved and take pride in our progress. By embracing imperfect action, setting realistic goals, and practicing self-compassion, we can break free from the cycle of guilt and shame and find a sense of calm and control in our work. Remember, it's okay to have a never-ending to-do list - it means we're ambitious and driven. And when we take care of ourselves and prioritize our well-being, we're better able to tackle those tasks with creativity, focus, and joy. So, let's give ourselves a break, shall we? We're doing the best we can, and that's something to be proud of.

253

Part 4

Communication and Relationships

Chapter 32

Shining in the Virtual Spotlight: Tips for Commanding an Online Presence

In today's world, so much of our communication and interaction takes place online. From video conferences for work to virtual hangouts with friends, many of our conversations and connections happen virtually. This means it's more important than ever to learn how to communicate effectively through a screen.

Just like performance artists command the stage with their presence, we can learn to shine in the virtual spotlight. The principles for engaging online conversations are actually quite similar to those used by actors on the stage. By framing your camera strategically, modulating your voice, using expressive facial expressions, and staying present in the moment, you can captivate your virtual audience.

In this chapter, we will explore tips for shining in the virtual world, so you can engage more effectively in online conversations and video calls. Drawing from techniques used by performance artists on the stage, these tips will help you improve your on-screen presence.

Framing the Screen

One of the most basic but impactful things you can do is pay attention to how you frame yourself on the screen. Carefully consider the backdrop, camera angle, lighting, and how you position yourself in the frame. This is similar to how a performance artist thinks about their positioning on the stage.

Some key tips for framing yourself on camera:

- Background - Choose a solid, neutral wall if possible, and remove clutter from the background. A plain backdrop keeps the focus on you.

- Camera angle - Position your camera at eye level or slightly above for a flattering perspective. Looking down at the camera can be unappealing.

- Lighting - Face a window or use a lamp to illuminated your face. Avoid having a bright light source behind you.

- Costume - Dress professionally from the waist up since that's primarily what's visible. Solid color shirts generally look best on camera.

- Framing - Position yourself close enough to the camera so your face and shoulders are fully in view. Maintain good posture and lean slightly towards the camera to appear engaged.

Use these tips to set up a professional, flattering on-screen framing. Pay the same attention to your virtual background as a performer does in positioned themselves on stage. A thoughtful, intentional frame brings focus to you and your message.

Modulating Your Voice

Your voice is your instrument for connecting with others online. Just as performers do vocal warm ups before a show, you can warm up your voice before video calls or presentations.

Some tips for improving your vocal presence:

- Before hopping on a call, take a few minutes to do some vocal exercises. Humming, lip trills, and tongue twisters can relax your vocal cords.

- Drink water and avoid dairy before speaking to keep your throat lubricated. Consider having tea or lemon water nearby to sip.

- Check your microphone volume before joining a call. You want the volume loud enough to be heard clearly without distortion or echo.

- Use vocal variety and inflection as you speak. Avoid monotone by varying your pitch, volume, and speed. Pausing between sentences also adds impact.

- Enunciate and articulate words clearly. Don't mumble or speak too fast. Over-emphasize consonants for clarity.

- Add energy and warmth to your tone. A lively, enthusiastic voice engages listeners and builds rapport.

With preparation and practice, you can develop a smooth, expressive virtual speaking voice. Pay as much attention to your vocal delivery as a performer does when rehearsing for the big show. A well-modulated voice makes you shine online.

The Face: Your Canvas of Expression

Facial expressions and eye contact are key ways we convey emotions and connect with others. That's still true in the virtual world, even though we're looking at screens instead of real faces. Use your face as a canvas to express yourself more fully.

Consider these tips for boosting your facial presence:

- Make strong eye contact by looking directly at your camera when speaking. This simulates eye contact with others.

- Raise your eyebrows, nod, and use expressions to signal engagement in the conversation. A smiling, interested face brings energy.

- Allow your face to fully express emotions like excitement, empathy, or humor. Don't suppress your natural expressions.

- Avoid distracting mannerisms like excessive blinking or face touching. Be aware of subtle tics.

- Keep an upright head position. Slouching and looking down appears disengaged on camera.

- Stay near the center of the frame so your whole face is visible. Moving around can take you out of view.

Your facial expressions add essential emotional context in virtual conversations. Use your face as an actor does on stage - don't hold back. With practice, your facial presence will become a natural strength.

Staying Present in the Moment

Being fully mentally present during virtual interactions is critical for making authentic connections. Avoid multi-tasking and give your full attention to others on the call.

Here are some tips for being more present:

- Minimize distractions by closing unnecessary tabs and apps before joining a call. Disable notifications.

- Do some deep breathing or meditation to settle your mind before joining a call. Clear your headspace.

- Listen attentively without interruption when others speak. Don't just wait for your turn.

- Let conversations flow naturally instead of over-planning what you'll say. React in the moment.

- Read nonverbal cues like facial expressions to gauge reactions. Adapt your style accordingly.

- If you feel distracted, refocus by making eye contact with the camera or asking a question.

Staying engaged and in-the-moment makes virtual interactions more natural. Don't let your attention drift - treat each call like a live performance requiring your full focus. With practice, you can achieve the same level of energetic presence online as you would in person.

Conclusion

Shining in online conversations requires adapting many techniques used by performance artists on the live stage. Consider how you frame yourself on camera, warm up and modulate your voice, use your face for expressive impact, and stay mentally present. With preparation and practice, you can command attention and connect with audiences virtually.

Bring your best, most vibrant self to video calls and online interactions. Project confidence through your voice, expressions and postures. Listen attentively and react naturally to others. By following principles used by actors on the stage, you'll consistently shine in the virtual spotlight. The online world is your platform - own it.

Chapter 33

Navigating Ageism in the Workplace: Strategies for Young Professionals

As a young professional, you bring a unique set of skills and perspectives to the workplace. However, despite your contributions, you may face a common challenge: ageism. Ageism, or discrimination based on age, can affect anyone, and young adults can experience it, just like older workers.

In this chapter, we will explore strategies for navigating ageism and ensuring that your voice is heard.

Start or Join a Working Group for Young Professionals

One of the most effective ways to combat ageism is to create a safe space where you can discuss your experiences with people you trust. Consider starting or joining a working group for young professionals in your organization. This group can provide a platform for you to share your concerns, receive support, and work together to address ageism.

For example, a group of young professionals at a tech company noticed that they were often excluded from important meetings and projects. They decided to form a working group to address this issue and other age-related challenges. They met regularly to share their experiences, provide support, and work together to advocate for their rights. As a result, they were able to effect change in their organization and create a more inclusive work environment.

Talk to Your Manager

Your manager may not be aware of the ageism you are facing, and they may have the power to help you navigate the situation. Consider scheduling a meeting with your manager to discuss your concerns. Be specific about the experiences you have had and how they have affected your work.

For example, a young professional named Sarah noticed that her ideas were often dismissed in meetings. She decided to talk to her manager about the issue. Her manager was surprised to hear about the problem and offered to help Sarah address it. Together, they came up with a plan to encourage more diverse perspectives in meetings. As a result, Sarah felt more valued and included in the team.

Have an Open Discussion with the Culprit

It's important to remember that not everyone who engages in ageist behavior does so intentionally. Sometimes, people may be unaware of the impact their words or actions have on others. If you feel comfortable, consider having an open discussion with the coworker who is demonstrating discrimination against you. Be respectful and specific about how their behavior has affected you.

For example, a young professional named Alex was consistently excluded from social events by a coworker who thought he was "too young" to participate. Alex decided to talk to the coworker and explained how his actions made him feel. The coworker was surprised and apologetic, and he made an effort to include Alex in future events.

Never Forget Your Value Add

It's important to remember that you bring a special skillset to the office, which is why you were hired. Don't let ageism undermine your confidence or make you feel like you don't belong. Instead, focus on your strengths and the value you bring to your team.

For example, a young professional named Emily was tasked with leading a project. Despite her qualifications, a colleague questioned her ability to lead due to her age. Emily decided to focus on her strengths and the skills she brought to the project. She worked hard, and her efforts paid off. The project was a success, and her colleagues recognized her value.

Conclusion

Ageism is a common challenge that young professionals may face in the workplace. However, by creating a safe space to discuss your experiences, talking to your manager, having an open discussion with the culprit, and remembering your value add, you can navigate these challenges and ensure that your voice is heard. Remember, you bring a unique set of skills and perspectives to the workplace. Don't let ageism hold you back from reaching your full potential.

269

Chapter 34

Getting Things Done Between Meetings

Meetings are an inevitable part of most workplaces. While meetings can be useful for collaboration, planning, and decision-making, they also take time away from other important work tasks. For many professionals, meetings make it challenging to find enough uninterrupted time to complete projects and other to-do list items. However, with some strategic planning, it is possible to get things done between meetings.

In this chapter, we will explore how to be productive with your to-do list when you have frequent meetings and provide examples and additional tips for prioritizing your tasks, breaking down projects, scheduling work time, and staying focused when you do have time between meetings. With some thoughtful preparation and time management, you can avoid constantly pushing tasks to another day and still find opportunities to make progress on your goals.

Getting Stuff Done When You Have Lots of Meetings

Here is some practical advice for professionals who struggle to complete their to-do lists and other important tasks because they spend so much time in meetings. While meetings are unavoidable in most jobs, you should not wait for the perfect, uninterrupted work day to get things done.

Instead, try the following:

- Break larger tasks down into smaller, manageable pieces that can be tackled between meetings.

- Proactively schedule blocks of work time into your calendar for project tasks. Try to protect these blocks as much as possible.

- Prioritize your tasks so you know what to focus on during any time you have between meetings.

- Don't let meetings entirely sabotage your productivity. With strategic planning, you can still make progress.

By approaching your to-do list in this more incremental, planned manner, you can avoid feeling like meetings derail your ability to get things done.

Expanding on Key Strategies

Professionals who want to improve their productivity between meetings should consider the following:

Schedule Work Time Strategically

- Block off longer stretches of time for tasks that require deeper focus. For example, schedule 2-3 hour blocks for working on a complex report or presentation.

- Take advantage of parts of the day when you tend to be most productive, like first thing in the morning.

- Schedule work time right before/after meetings you already have booked.

- Cluster meetings together to create longer stretches of open time on your calendar.

Prioritize Ruthlessly

- Rank your tasks by importance and deadline to focus on top priorities first.

- Within a project, start with steps that will have the biggest impact.

- Schedule time-consuming tasks for when you have longer open blocks.

- Be willing to reschedule lower priority tasks if needed.

Get a Head Start

- Try to get the ball rolling on projects even if you only have 15 minutes. Outline the presentation or start gathering research.

- Process emails and to-dos right after meetings while the discussions are still fresh.

- Spend the last 5 minutes of a meeting planning what you'll work on immediately after.

Limit Distractions

- Silence notifications and close unneeded apps and browser tabs.

- Block time on your calendar to focus if needed.

- Let colleagues know when you are heads-down on a project and should not be disturbed.

Work in Small Chunks

- Break down large goals into single tasks that can be tackled in 15-30 minutes.

- Use tools like Trello to create checklists you can quickly work through.

- Keep track of what you accomplish between meetings so you can easily pick up where you left off.

Have Transitional Rituals

- After finishing a meeting, take 2 minutes to review notes, update your to-do list, and shift gears.

- Between meetings, set a timer for 5 minutes of deep breathing or meditation to refresh your focus.

- Maintain energy by taking a short walk outside or stretching.

By combining these types of strategies, you can make steady progress chipping away at your goals and priorities, no matter how scattered your days are. The key is having structure and intention in how you use the time that is available. With practice, you can learn to avoid procrastination and stay laser-focused even during short blocks of time between meetings.

Application Examples

To further illustrate how these techniques can work, let's walk through some detailed examples:

Example 1: John has a presentation he needs to create for an upcoming regional sales meeting. Rather than wait until he has a full day with no meetings to dedicate to it, he breaks the project down into specific chunks:

- Research market data and trends (1 hour)

- Write section covering current sales statistics (30 mins)

- Complete intro slides with agenda (20 mins)

- Write notes for main presentation content (1.5 hours)

- Revise/edit slides (1 hour)

He schedules 60-90 minutes time slots over the next two weeks to work through each chunk between his recurring update and planning meetings.

Example 2: Alicia has a long list of tasks that includes everything from finishing expense reports to contacting new clients. She ranks them by priority, putting time-sensitive deliverables like the client outreach at the top. She also groups related tasks, like batching administrative items she can tackle efficiently together.

When she has any open time slot of 25 minutes or more between meetings, she picks the top uncompleted item from her ranked list to work on. This ensures she makes the best use of the limited time she has available.

Example 3: Marcus has recurring meetings Mondays and Wednesdays. He schedules focused work time on his calendar Tuesday and Thursday mornings. Before each meeting block, he reviews his tasks and goals and plans what he wants to accomplish during that block. He gathers any relevant materials and jumps straight into the planned task right after each meeting ends to maintain momentum.

Conclusion

Professionals today inevitably spend a lot of their time in meetings. While meetings can make it challenging to find time for independent work, with intentional planning it is possible to be productive between meetings. Break down larger goals into doable chunks. Prioritize ruthlessly. Schedule work time strategically around your meetings. Limit distractions and transition purposefully from meetings to focused work. If you leverage all the small bits of time between meetings, you can avoid the endless frustration of a mounting to-do list and steadily make progress, even on your busiest days. With some practice, you can learn to thrive within the reality of frequent meetings.

279

BUILDING HIGH-PERFORMING ORGANIZATIONS

Chapter 35

Recognizing and Responding to Manipulation in Workplace Relationships

Influence and manipulation may seem similar on the surface, but there are important distinctions between these interpersonal dynamics. While influence refers to having an effect on someone's actions or beliefs, manipulation involves the use of deception, exploitation, and other unethical tactics to control someone.

In this chapter, we will explore the differences between influence and manipulation, provide examples of manipulative behaviors, and offer strategies for protecting oneself from manipulation in relationships at work.

Defining Influence versus Manipulation

Influence refers to the general capacity to sway another person's thinking or behavior. Influence itself is neutral - it can be used for positive or negative ends. Teachers influence students to learn, friends influence each other to make healthy choices, and parents influence children's values. In contrast, manipulation refers to the use of sneaky, abusive, or otherwise unethical tactics to control someone. While influence creates change through persuasion, manipulation creates change through coercion, exploitation, or deceit.

There are several key differences between influence and manipulation:

- Intent: The intent behind influence is to benefit the person being influenced, or at minimum do no harm. The manipulator's intent is to benefit themselves, often at the other person's expense.

- Tactics: Influence relies on logical reasoning, inspiration, and ethical persuasion methods. Manipulation relies on inducing fear, doubt, guilt, or other emotional states to overpower the person's reason.

- Transparency: Influence is overt, direct, and transparent. Manipulation relies on covert, indirect, deceptive tactics.

- Consent: The targets of influence consent to the process of being influenced. Manipulation is non-consensual and resists the target's right to choose their own path.

- Outcome: Influence enhances a person's autonomy and improves their decision-making. Manipulation reduces personal autonomy and harms well-being.

Examples of Manipulative Behaviors

Now let's explore several examples of manipulative tactics:

- *Gaslighting:* Manipulators will outright deny factual realities, causing targets to distrust their own memory and perception. For example, an abusive partner may vehemently deny verbally insulting their spouse, making the spouse question whether the hurtful incident occurred.

- *Lying:* Manipulators may outright lie about any number of things to control the target's beliefs and behaviors. For example, a manager may lie about a coworker's poor performance as part of a ploy to get the coworker demoted or fired.

- *Guilt-tripping:* By inducing excessive feelings of guilt and obligation, manipulators coerce targets into doing things they would not freely choose to do. For example, a parent may excessively guilt-trip an adult child into providing lavish financial support.

- *Love bombing:* Manipulators shower the target with over-the-top praise and affection to quickly establish control, only to later withdraw it to induce compliance. For example, cult leaders will love bomb new recruits with extreme warmth initially.

- *Silent treatment:* By ignoring the target as punishment for perceived disobedience, manipulators train the target to comply with their wishes. For example, a friend may give another friend the silent treatment for spending time with other peers.

Protecting Yourself from Manipulation

It is important to pay attention to emotional cues and behavioral patterns as a way to detect manipulation, including the following strategies:

- Notice when someone resists your attempts to make your own choices or assert your boundaries. Manipulators need control.

- Pay attention when interactions leave you feeling confused, distrustful of your own judgment, excessively guilty, or dependent on the other person's approval. These are signs of manipulation.

- Consider whether there are double standards at play or the person contradicts themselves. Hypocrisy and inconsistencies are red flags.

- Watch for gaslighting techniques like outright lying, denying factual realities, or insisting you said or did things you know you didn't.

- Reflect on whether the person expresses concern for your needs and desires, or disregards them. Manipulators are selfish.

- Ask someone you trust for an outside perspective on the relationship dynamics. Manipulators try to isolate their targets.

By identifying manipulative behaviors early and resisting their tactics, you can protect your emotional, psychological, and relational health. Maintaining strong boundaries and self-confidence are your best defenses.

Conclusion

While influence and manipulation may appear similar on the surface, there are crucial differences. Influence is ethically neutral and can be beneficial, while manipulation is unethical and causes harm. Manipulators rely on tactics like gaslighting, guilt-tripping, lying, and denial to control their targets. To protect yourself, become aware of the warning signs, listen to your emotional cues, gain outside perspective, and maintain firm personal boundaries against coercion and exploitation. With insight, confidence, and assertiveness, you can stand strong in the face of manipulation and make choices aligned with your values.

287

Chapter 36

Why Family and Domestic Violence Is a Workplace Issue

Family and domestic violence (FDV) is often viewed as a private matter that only affects the individuals directly involved. However, FDV has far-reaching impacts that extend into the workplace. Employees who are victims of FDV may experience chronic absenteeism, decreased productivity, and safety concerns that affect their work performance. As a manager, it is important to understand how FDV can manifest in the workplace and learn strategies to support affected employees.

In this chapter, we will summarize key points on why FDV is a workplace issue, provide detailed examples, and offer recommendations for managers to address FDV at work.

Understanding How FDV Impacts the Workplace

FDV can negatively impact employees and the workplace in several ways. Victims may have difficulty concentrating, experience fatigue, or require time off to handle legal issues, medical appointments, or find housing solutions. This can lead to absenteeism, tardiness, and reduced quality of work. Victims may also receive harassing phone calls or emails from their abuser at work, causing disruptions. Coworkers may witness aggressive behavior from the abuser dropping by the workplace. Experiencing trauma from FDV causes significant stress that hinders an employee's optimal performance. FDV also affects the bottom line for employers through lost productivity and increased health care costs.

Some warning signs that an employee may be experiencing FDV include:

- Visible bruising or injuries with vague explanations

- Changes in job performance - missing deadlines, mistakes, distracted

- Frequent absenteeism, especially Monday/Friday or without notice

- Isolation from coworkers and declining participation in work events

- Receiving excessive personal calls/emails that cause distress

- Disruptive visits to the workplace by a partner or family member

A victim of FDV may turn to drugs or alcohol to cope, violating workplace policies. They may also be unable to leave their partner due to financial dependence, which could prevent them from performing work duties like traveling for projects. Managers should be aware of these potential red flags and address changes in behavior or performance issues sensitively. Assuming poor work ethic without considering potential FDV can further isolate an affected employee.

Legal Obligations

Managers should be informed on laws regarding FDV in the workplace. In the U.S., some key federal and state regulations include:

- *Title VII of the Civil Rights Act* - prohibits employment discrimination based on sex, which includes FDV. Employers can be held liable for allowing a hostile work environment.

- *The Occupational Safety and Health Act* - requires employers to provide a safe workplace. This includes preventing harassment, threats, and harm from perpetrators.

- *State Domestic Violence Leave Laws* - provide job-protected leave for employees to obtain help with FDV situations. Many states have implemented such laws with varying requirements.

- *State Unemployment Insurance Laws* - allow domestic violence victims who voluntarily leave employment for safety reasons to receive unemployment benefits.

- *Workplace Restraining Orders* - available in some states to prohibit abusers from contacting or approaching victims at work. Employers must comply with approved orders.

Understanding relevant laws shows managers how failure to address FDV can lead to liability risks for the company. It also clarifies what protections are legally afforded to victims.

Advocating for Stronger Policies

Managers play a key role in advocating for more robust FDV policies within their organization. Here are some ways managers can promote a supportive workplace:

- Review current policies and procedures related to FDV. Are they adequate? Make suggestions on improvements to HR.

- Encourage HR to conduct FDV training for all employees to increase awareness. Volunteer to participate.

- Ask about implementing leave policies that provide paid time off for addressing FDV issues.

- Suggest flexible work arrangements that could help victims safely separate from abusers, such as telecommuting or transfer options.

- Share educational resources on FDV with leadership and request communication be sent out on workplace policies.

- Organize a fundraiser to support local domestic violence programs. Get leadership to match contributions.

- Work with security personnel to develop safety plans, such as alerting staff if an abuser enters premises.

- Promote an employee assistance program (EAP) that offers FDV counseling services.

By championing these types of initiatives, managers give victims greater flexibility and resources to seek help while also protecting employer interests.

Fostering a Supportive Work Culture

Managers set the tone for workplace culture. Here are some tips on how to build a supportive team environment:

- Train staff on recognizing signs of FDV and appropriate responses. Ensure they know policies around confidentiality and non-discrimination.

- Make resources readily available, like posters with the national domestic violence hotline number or listing local services.

- If an employee discloses FDV, listen with empathy, reiterate confidentiality, and share company policies on support options. Avoid pressuring them to take specific actions.

- In team discussions, use inclusive language like "partner" instead of "husband/wife" and don't make assumptions about relationships.

- Intervene sensitively if employees make inappropriate jokes about FDV. Explain the impacts and that humor normalizes violence.

- Allow flexible schedules or remote work for employees facing safety issues. Don't require them to disclose personal details.

- Adjust performance standards temporarily and avoid penalties against victims. Understand trauma can affect work quality.

- Be prepared to report any threats made against employees by outside parties to security staff. Take preventive measures.

Creating a workplace where victims feel safe to get support without judgment is key. FDV should be treated seriously, with the understanding it can happen to anyone.

Conclusion

FDV profoundly impacts employees and places of work. Managers have an important role in addressing this issue by knowing legal obligations, advocating for strong policies, and fostering a supportive culture. Victims' safety and wellbeing should be the top priority. With the right response, workplaces can become part of the solution to ending the cycles of violence instead of ignoring the problem. Implementing best practices around FDV makes for more informed, adaptable, and high-functioning work environments. Above all, displaying compassion and flexibility will allow affected employees to get the help they need to regain their footing, both personally and professionally.

297

Chapter 37

Finding the Balance: How to Be Direct Without Being Rude

In today's fast-paced business environment, it's essential for leaders to be direct and straightforward in their communication. However, being too blunt can come across as rude and abrasive, which can negatively impact team morale and relationships. The key is to find a healthy balance between being direct and being considerate.

In this chapter, we will explore some practical tips for leaders to communicate effectively without being perceived as rude or aggressive.

Talk Facts, Not Emotions

When giving feedback, it's essential to focus on facts rather than emotions. Facts are objective and provide a clear picture of what needs improvement. Emotions, on the other hand, are subjective and can be misinterpreted or misconstrued. By sticking to facts, you're not only being more considerate but also providing concrete evidence for the person to improve.

For instance, instead of saying, "Your presentation was terrible," say, "I noticed that you didn't provide enough examples to support your points. Next time, could you include more case studies to strengthen your argument?" This approach removes personal emotions from the conversation and focuses on specific areas for improvement.

Use "I" Statements, Not "You" Statements

When expressing an opinion, it's important to use "I" statements instead of "you" statements. Accusatory language can quickly shut down a conversation or escalate it into an argument. "You" statements come across as finger-pointing and can make the receiver defensive.

For example, instead of saying, "You always miss the deadline," say, "I've noticed that the project has been delayed several times. Can we discuss possible ways to meet the deadline in the future?" This approach allows you to express your concerns without placing blame or pointing fingers.

Turn a "No" into a Soft "Yes"

When someone asks you for something, it's natural to want to say "no" when you're busy or overwhelmed. However, a flat-out "no" can come across as unhelpful or uncooperative. Instead, try turning a "no" into a soft "yes" by offering an alternative solution.

For example, "I understand that you need help with this project, but I don't have the bandwidth to take it on right now. However, I can introduce you to someone who might be able to assist you, or I can provide some guidance on how to approach the project." This approach shows that you're willing to help while also being considerate of your own workload.

Be Considerate, Not Commanding

When making a request, it's important to be considerate of the other person's time and workload. Avoid being bossy or demanding, as this can create resentment and undermine trust. Instead, show appreciation for the person's help and time.

For example, "I need your help with a project, and I know you're busy. I appreciate any time you can spare, and I'll make sure to provide all the necessary information to make it as easy as possible for you." This approach shows that you value the person's contributions and are willing to work together to achieve a common goal.

Conclusion

Finding the balance between being direct and being considerate is a delicate art. By talking facts, using "I" statements, turning a "no" into a soft "yes," and being considerate in your requests, you can communicate effectively without coming across as rude or abrasive. Remember that clear communication is essential for efficiency and productivity, but it's equally important to be mindful of how your words and actions impact others. With practice and patience, you can develop a leadership style that is both direct and considerate, leading to stronger relationships and better outcomes for your team and organization.

Chapter 38

When "I'm Sorry" Goes Too Far: Learning to Apologize Effectively at Work

Apologizing is an important part of maintaining positive relationships at work. When we make a mistake that negatively impacts a coworker or fails to meet expectations, taking ownership and apologizing is the right thing to do. However, incessantly saying "I'm sorry" for every minor misstep can diminish an apology's meaning and have unintended consequences.

In this chapter, we will explore advice on avoiding over-apologizing at work and learning to apologize effectively. Key points include understanding the roots of over-apologizing, knowing when an apology is truly warranted, and delivering meaningful apologies that rebuild trust and respect. Tactics for curbing the urge to apologize unnecessarily are also provided.

The Risks of Over-Apologizing

Over-apologizing refers to saying "sorry" reflexively, even when an apology is unwarranted. This tendency stems from various sources:

- Low self-confidence: Those with imposter syndrome and self-doubt may over-apologize due to feeling insecure or undeserving.

- Desire to please: Some compulsively apologize to avoid conflict or earn others' approval at all costs.

- Perfectionism: Holding oneself to impossibly high standards leads some to apologize for any perceived mistake or inadequacy.

While the intention is to be polite and accountable, excessive apologies can undermine professionalism and credibility. Coworkers may stop taking apologies seriously or view constant apologizers as incompetent. Over-apologizing also continues negative thought patterns like perfectionism.

In short, incessant sorries distort the purpose of a sincere apology: taking ownership of mistakes and re-earning trust through changed behavior. As author Laresha Franks explains, "Apologizing should serve to mend bonds, not break you."

Knowing When to Apologize

The first step in more effective apologies is understanding appropriate situations. Apologies at work are warranted when an action (or lack thereof) creates tangible negative impacts, such as:

- Missed deadlines or expectations due to errors

- Poor quality work necessitating revisions

- Overlooking tasks that affect coworkers' workloads

- Publicly losing one's temper and being disrespectful

In contrast, minor mistakes that primarily impact only you do not require an apology.

Examples include:

- Arriving a few minutes late to a meeting that proceeds normally

- Needing clarification on instructions or expectations

- Respectfully advocating an alternate viewpoint in a discussion

Additionally, do not apologize for non-errors like requesting time off or declining invites to non-mandatory events. You have nothing to be sorry for – state your reasons respectfully without apologies.

Finally, do not reflexively apologize for positive steps like giving critical feedback to help others improve. Frame feedback professionally as doing your job, not something requiring forgiveness.

Crafting Meaningful Apologies

All apologies should contain these core elements:

- *Sincerity*: Apologize only for actions you are genuinely remorseful for, not just to appease others.

- *Accountability*: Avoid excuses by succinctly stating what you did wrong and taking full responsibility.

- *Impact*: Acknowledge how your actions negatively affected coworkers, clients, or the company. Be specific.

- *Change*: Explain how you will prevent a repeat mistake or address any ongoing issues created.

- *Request for forgiveness*: Ask if the person is willing to accept your apology without pressuring them to.

Additionally, apologies for major mistakes should take place quickly in private conversations. Smaller errors may warrant a simple "my apologies" email. Format apologies appropriately for the audience and severity.

Being solutions-oriented also boosts apologies. Rather than just admitting failure, state how you plan to get projects back on track and what support you need. For public outbursts, apologize privately then lead visibly positive behavior going forward.

Curtailing Over-Apologizing

Breaking the over-apology habit requires mindset shifts:

- *Focus on actions, not anxieties.* Ask yourself – did I make an actual error that contributed to a negative outcome? If not, an apology adds no value.

- *Remember apologies' purpose.* They should address harms, not serve as verbal tics.

- *Balance perfectionism with reality.* You will make some mistakes – do not apologize for being human.

- *Be resolute, not stubborn.* Tactfully stand by justifiable decisions without defensiveness.

- *Own your worth.* You deserve to be at work as much as any coworker. Do not apologize for taking up space.

- *Ask yourself "would I apologize to a friend?"* Treat yourself with that same compassion.

With practice, you can learn to apologize only when meaningful while maintaining professionalism and self-assurance. The result is apologies that rebuild trust and respect without self-deprecation.

Conclusion

Apologizing well is a workplace skill. While overly-frequent sorries seem polite, they diminish apologies' significance and paint an unflattering image of low confidence. With guidance on when an apology is truly warranted and how to apologize effectively, professionals can showcase accountability without self-denigration. Curtail over-apologies by focusing only on substantive harms and delivering solutions-focused apologies that genuinely reconnect. Learn to say sorry only when it counts.

Part 5

Innovation and Change Management

Chapter 39

Beyond Stage-Gate: New Approaches to Managing Breakthrough Innovation Projects

The stage-gate process has long been a staple of product development, providing structure and governance to take ideas from conception to launch. However, this linear, milestone-driven approach falls short when it comes to breakthrough innovations that aim to profoundly shift human behaviors. Companies like BMW and Air France have pioneered new management frameworks better suited to handle the ambiguity and unpredictability inherent in driving transformational change.

In this chapter, we will explore the limitations of the stage-gate model for breakthrough projects and detail some of the alternative frameworks companies are using to nurture game-changing ideas.

The Stage-Gate Shortcomings

The traditional stage-gate process divides product development into discrete stages separated by go/no-go gates. This provides discipline to funnel out weak ideas and helps managers track progress. However, it relies on a linear execution plan defined upfront when uncertainties are highest. Breakthrough innovations that attempt to fundamentally shift customer behaviors have murkier requirements and feedback loops. They involve greater technological and adoption risks that make their pathways unpredictable. Rigid stage-gate processes struggle to adapt to the inevitable changes in direction these projects require.

BMW's Adaptive Framework

Recognizing these limitations, BMW has developed a more flexible project management framework for their radical i3 electric vehicle. They divide the initiative into areas focused on key questions like technology feasibility, usage patterns, and manufacturing. Work streams within these areas iterate rapidly to test hypotheses and evolve the concepts. The overall project coordinates across these streams but remains nimble to adjustments as learning occurs. Rather than preset timelines, BMW manages based on achievement of key milestones or 'maturity gates' that demonstrate proof of concept and readiness to proceed. This empowers teams to adapt tactics while driving toward the strategic vision.

Air France's Minimum Viable Experience

Air France faced a significant challenge in shifting customer habits toward self-service check-in. Their approach focused on quickly building a 'minimum viable experience' that provided core functionality, then iteratively refining it based on customer feedback. This allowed them to fail fast and cheaply on initial concepts and build knowledge of what worked. They rolled the evolving product out incrementally so they could isolate and address issues. By embracing setbacks as learning opportunities not failures, they were able to successfully adapt the product until it reached broad adoption. This experimentation-driven process provided flexibility missing from rigid stage-gate models.

Principles for Managing Breakthroughs

These examples illustrate ways companies are reinventing project management for transformational innovation. Some key principles that enable this include:

- Divide initiatives into rapid iterative work streams around key questions or capabilities, not preset stages and gates

- Develop minimum viable versions to start learning quickly, guide evolution

- Manage to strategic milestones based on demonstrated knowledge, not timelines

- Test hypotheses early and often, make adjustments as learnings dictate

- Implement incrementally to isolate issues and build adoption momentum

- View setbacks as data to adapt and improve, not failures

- Engage a broad community and co-create with customers to build insights

- Maintain transparency and shared purpose to enable autonomy and agility

These practices require managers to take on new roles as vision-setters, coordinators, and facilitators who empower teams to adapt based on learnings. They represent a profound shift from controlling rigid plans.

Conclusion

The unpredictability of breakthrough innovations demands project management approaches that embrace uncertainty and evolution. Clinging to the linear stage-gate model only handicaps efforts to drive transformational change. Leaders must be willing to trade false security of detailed plans for the flexibility to nurture game-changing ideas. With the future landscape sure to bring increasing disruption, adopting these exploratory project management principles will only grow in importance. Companies that cling to rigid practices do so at their peril.

Chapter 40

Using the Zeigarnik Effect to Your Advantage

The Zeigarnik effect, named after psychologist Bluma Zeigarnik, refers to the tendency of the human mind to remember unfinished or interrupted tasks better than completed tasks. According to Zeigarnik's research in the 1920s, people have a better recollection of tasks that were started but not finished, compared to tasks that were completed. This occurs because an unfinished task creates tension and activation in the mind that makes details about the task more memorable. Once the task is completed, this tension is released and the details start fading from memory.

The Zeigarnik effect has important implications in our lives. It explains why we often feel bothered by unfinished projects and tend to procrastinate on completing tasks. However, instead of viewing it as an intrusion, we can use the Zeigarnik effect to our advantage in several ways.

Today we will summarize the key points about the Zeigarnik effect and provide detailed examples of how to harness it to become more productive, improve memorization, captivate audiences, and remember people's names.

Using Zeigarnik to Overcome Procrastination

One of the most common manifestations of the Zeigarnik effect is procrastination. When we put off finishing a task, it weighs on our mind more heavily compared to completed tasks. This underlying tension is what motivates us to eventually complete the task in order to get closure.

To overcome procrastination, we can use the Zeigarnik effect by intentionally leaving tasks unfinished. For example, when writing a long report, intentionally completing just the introduction and outline before taking a break. Since the incomplete report will occupy your mind more, you will be eager to return to it faster. Breaking large projects into smaller incomplete chunks makes them less overwhelming.

You can also combat procrastination by turning a long-term goal into a series of incomplete tasks. If your goal is to lose 20 pounds, break it into smaller 5-pound milestones. Celebrate and reward each partial completion, while the unfinished goal continues motivating you. This way you get the satisfaction of progress plus the nagging of the Zeigarnik effect.

Improving Memorization with Zeigarnik

The Zeigarnik effect also has powerful implications for improving memory and recall. According to research, interrupted or incomplete tasks are remembered up to 90% better compared to completed tasks.

To harness this, when trying to memorize information like a speech, intentionally stop rehearsing before fully memorizing it. Your memory will subconsciously dwell on the unfinished rehearsal, helping you memorize the speech better for the next practice session.

You can also leverage the Zeigarnik effect when memorizing long lists or definitions. Memorize the first half of the list, then take a break. Your mind will retain that incomplete information better. Then memorize the full list during your next study session for optimal recall. Breaking the memorization into unfinished chunks capitalizes on the Zeigarnik effect.

Captivating Audiences with Zeigarnik

Speakers can also use the Zeigarnik effect to get audiences more engaged in their content. When giving a presentation, introduce topics but leave some points unfinished. You can tease future ideas without fully explaining them yet.

Since unfinished ideas create intrigue and tension, the audience will stay focused in anticipation of the complete details coming later. You can also share stories but leave out the endings to pique curiosity. Just be sure to satisfy the audience's craving for closure eventually. Employing this effect strategically keeps them hooked from start to finish.

Remembering Names Using Zeigarnik

Finally, the Zeigarnik effect can be applied when you want to better remember someone's name. When you first get introduced to someone, intentionally avoid repeating their name right away. That incomplete knowledge of their name will keep circulating in your mind, helping you solidify the memory.

You can also strengthen the Zeigarnik effect by associating the unfinished name with the person's physical features or conversation details. This acts like a mental cue that keeps nagging you to fully complete the memory with their name. Once you finally do repeat their name out loud, the satisfaction of closure will lock it into your memory for good.

Conclusion

While the Zeigarnik effect can lead to procrastination and intrusive thoughts, we can take advantage of it to boost productivity, memory, public speaking skills, and relationship-building. By strategically interrupting tasks and leaving things partially unfinished, we can prime our minds to focus on processing and retaining the unfinished information. Completing the task then provides satisfying closure. With some diligence, we can use this quirk in human psychology to our benefit in various life and work domains. The key is transforming the Zeigarnik effect from a subconscious annoyance into a deliberate mental tool.

Chapter 41

Unlocking Dynamism: Understanding Common Keys to Successful Companies

In today's fast-paced business landscape, staying ahead of the curve is crucial for companies to remain competitive and relevant. While some organizations seem to effortlessly adapt to changing market conditions and customer preferences, others struggle to keep up. The question is, what sets these dynamic companies apart from the rest?

In this chapter, we will explore the key factors that contribute to a company's dynamism, and provide practical examples to help you understand and apply these principles in your own organization.

Embrace a Culture of Innovation

Dynamic companies foster a culture that encourages and rewards innovation. They create an environment where employees are free to think outside the box, experiment with new ideas, and take calculated risks. This culture of innovation allows them to stay ahead of the curve and capitalize on emerging trends.

For example, Google, known for its creative and innovative approach, has a dedicated team called X, which focuses on developing moonshot technologies, such as self-driving cars and augmented reality glasses. This team is given the freedom to explore new ideas and technologies, and their work has led to several groundbreaking inventions.

Foster Collaboration and Communication

Dynamic companies understand the importance of collaboration and communication. They create a work environment where employees can share ideas, provide feedback, and work together towards a common goal. This helps to foster a sense of unity and encourages creative problem-solving.

Atlassian, an Australian software company, has a "FedEx Day" once a quarter, where employees are given 24 hours to work on any project they want, as long as it's delivered within the time frame. This encourages collaboration, creativity, and innovation, and has led to several successful products and features.

Be Adaptable and Resilient

Dynamic companies are adaptable and resilient, meaning they can quickly respond to changes in the market and bounce back from setbacks. They have a flexible organizational structure that allows them to pivot when necessary and capitalize on new opportunities.

For example, Netflix, once a DVD rental service, adapted to the shift towards streaming and now produces original content that caters to a global audience. This adaptability has allowed them to maintain their position as a market leader.

Focus on Customer Experience

Dynamic companies prioritize customer experience and continuously gather feedback to improve their products and services. They understand that customer satisfaction is key to building brand loyalty and driving growth.

Airbnb, a platform that connects travelers with local hosts, has a user-centric approach that focuses on creating unique and personalized experiences. They gather feedback from both hosts and guests to continually improve their platform and services.

Invest in Employee Development

Dynamic companies invest in employee development, recognizing that their workforce is their greatest asset. They provide training, mentorship, and opportunities for growth, which not only benefits the employee but also the company as a whole.

For example, LinkedIn, a professional networking platform, offers a range of training courses and resources for employees, as well as a "Learning and Development" program that allows employees to dedicate 10% of their worktime to learning new skills.

Conclusion

Dynamic companies possess certain key characteristics that set them apart from their less agile counterparts. By fostering a culture of innovation, collaboration, and communication, being adaptable and resilient, prioritizing customer experience, and investing in employee development, these companies are able to stay ahead of the curve and achieve long-term success. By studying and applying these principles, your organization can also unlock its dynamism and achieve greater heights.

Chapter 42

Overcoming Imposter Syndrome: Turning Fear into Power

Starting a new job or taking on greater responsibility in your career can be extremely daunting. Imposter syndrome, the persistent feeling that you are a fraud and don't belong or aren't qualified despite evidence to the contrary, is incredibly common. In fact, an estimated 70% of people experience imposter syndrome at some point in their lives. However, imposter syndrome doesn't have to hold you back. With the right mindset and strategies, you can transform those fears into fuel to power you forward and achieve your goals.

Work Harder Than Anyone Else To Prove Yourself

When starting a new job or taking on a challenging new project, it's easy to feel like you don't measure up to your colleagues. You may worry that your coworkers will discover you don't know as much as they think you do. While some self-doubt is normal, don't let fear paralyze you. Instead, use it as motivation to work harder than anyone else. Establish yourself as the most diligent, detail-oriented, and dedicated employee. No matter how menial or boring the task, attack it with gusto. Doing the grunt work well demonstrates your commitment and earns you opportunities to take on more significant responsibilities.

Former NFL executive Mike Tannenbaum advised players, "How you do anything is how you do everything." This applies to all careers. Excel at mundane tasks, and people will have faith that you can handle more high-stakes projects. Pay attention to details that others overlook. Arrive early, stay late, ask thoughtful questions, and volunteer for extra assignments. By becoming indispensable through your work ethic, you prove that you belong and silence that inner critic questioning your abilities.

Invest in Yourself to Become More Prepared

Fear often stems from feeling unprepared. Rather than let it stop you in your tracks, use it as a call to action. Make a list of the skills, knowledge, or experience that would make you feel more equipped for the task or role causing you anxiety. Then get to work obtaining those things. This investment in yourself is well worth the effort. The more prepared you are, the more confident and empowered you will feel.

For example, if public speaking terrifies you, take a class on presentation skills. Seek out opportunities to practice speaking in low-stakes environments, like Toastmasters meetings. Read books on commanding an audience and managing stage fright. By actively working to improve your public speaking abilities, you will worry less about judgment. You'll have tangible skills to draw on instead of focusing on fear.

The same principle applies when taking on a daunting new project. Identify people who have successfully handled similar initiatives. Reach out and ask them for advice on recommended preparations. Use their guidance as a roadmap for getting up to speed quickly. The more proactive effort you put into getting ready, the less imposter syndrome can sabotage you.

Take Risks Now Rather Than Later

As much as imposter syndrome can hold us back from going after opportunities, so can waiting for the perfect moment. When considering a risky move like changing careers, starting a business, or accepting a promotion, it's tempting to delay until you feel 100% ready. But that time may never come. If you wait until you have mastered every necessary skill, the market may shift. Someone else may beat you to seizing the opportunity. Your life may become too rooted in your current path.

Rather than fixing imposter syndrome through avoidance, use the fear of standing still to propel yourself forward now. The truth is there will always be some degree of uncertainty and discomfort when taking on new challenges. You must be willing to tolerate those feelings to achieve your goals. Recognize that the riskiest move of all is standing in place out of fear. Have faith that you will figure things out as you go just like everyone else. Keep your eyes on the long-term vision of where you want to go.

Leverage Others' Expertise

One of the best ways to combat imposter syndrome is realizing you don't need to do everything alone. Find people who have already achieved what you want to do and leverage their expertise. Don't wait for them to offer help. Proactively seek out mentors and advisors you can learn from.

For example, if looking to start your own business, find entrepreneurs who have successfully built companies in your industry. Take them out for coffee to hear their stories. Ask about their biggest challenges and how they overcame obstacles. Apply their hard-won wisdom to your own venture. Stay humble and recognize that you can shortcut years of trial and error by learning from those who have done it before.

You can also hire experts to provide tactical guidance. If the legal aspects of launching a business intimidate you, work with a lawyer experienced in these matters. Let their knowledge remove hurdles and instill confidence. Surround yourself with people whose strengths complement your weaknesses. It takes courage to admit what you don't know, but the payoff is huge.

Conclusion

Imposter syndrome can make any career transition or challenge seem insurmountable. However, viewing fear as a stop sign limits your potential. With the right mindset and strategies, you can transform your self-doubt into rocket fuel. Have faith in your ability to rise to the occasion and silence the inner critic.

Work diligently to prove yourself. Invest time and effort into becoming as prepared as possible. Muster the courage to take risks now rather than later. Seek knowledge from those further along than you. The energy that fear takes from you, you can take back. Direct it into powering yourself toward your goals. The path to success is never going to feel wholly comfortable, but you are far more ready for it than you think.

Chapter 43

Reimagining the Managerial Pipeline for the 21st Century Workplace

Managers today face unprecedented challenges. With rapidly evolving technologies, business models, and worker expectations, managers must adapt and take on wide-ranging responsibilities to help their teams succeed. However, many struggle with the complexities of the role. A recent survey found that 54% of managers experience work-related stress and fatigue. Additionally, only half of employees believe their manager can effectively support the team. Clearly, there is room for improvement when it comes to equipping managers for success.

A new study from Gartner points to a critical starting point - putting the right people into management roles in the first place. Rather than promoting based on individual performance, organizations need a rigorous, anonymous selection process where people opt into management. With the right pipeline, managers are twice as likely to find the role manageable and lead higher-performing teams. By reimagining how managers are selected and developed, organizations can build a robust pipeline ready to step up when needed.

The Evolving Role of Management

Today's managers navigate a vastly more complex role than in decades past. They are expected to support workers' needs for flexibility and autonomy while also driving productivity and strategy implementation. Managers must make quick decisions with limited information. They need both hard skills like data analysis and soft skills like emotional intelligence. On top of it all, they deal with trying to motivate and engage team members who may be geographically dispersed or have differing work styles.

With these increasing demands, it's no wonder managers report struggling. The data shows 54% suffer from work-related stress and fatigue. Additionally, only 50% of employees say their manager can effectively help the team succeed. Expectations have expanded faster than managers have been equipped with new skills and support systems.

Rethinking the Manager Selection Process

To better prepare the next generation of managers, organizations need to rethink how managers get promoted in the first place. Historically, many have been promoted based on their individual performance as standout employees. However, the skills that make someone an excellent individual contributor don't necessarily translate to being an excellent manager.

According to Gartner's research, organizations need a more rigorous and anonymous selection process for management roles. Instead of managers nominating their favorites, any employee who's interested should be able to opt in and apply. An anonymous review of applications can help surface overlooked but promising candidates. Equipping candidates with realistic previews of the role's challenges can help them self-assess their fit. Structured interviews, assessments, and competency demonstrations can reveal who's best prepared to take on the role's diverse responsibilities.

This kind of process does more than find the most qualified candidates - it builds a robust, diverse pipeline of managers. When people opt into management, rather than being pushed into it, they're more engaged in developing leadership capabilities before formally taking on the role. This ultimately leads to higher-caliber managers who feel empowered in their work.

Preparing Managers to Succeed

With the right rigorous selection process, organizations will have a pipeline of qualified candidates for management positions. But putting someone in the role is just the first step. Organizations must also equip new managers with the skills, mindsets, and support systems to thrive.

Ongoing training is crucial, given how quickly business conditions change. Managers should regularly refresh their knowledge of technologies, regulations, and trends impacting their teams' work. Soft skills development is also important, including emotional intelligence, communication, relationship-building, and coaching skills. Organizations can use a combination of formal training programs, mentorships, peer groups, and real-time coaching to help managers continuously develop.

There also needs to be support systems to avoid manager burnout. New managers should have leadership check-ins to troubleshoot challenges and prevent feelings of isolation. Workloads and spans of control should be reasonable to prevent fatigue. Promoting work-life balance and modeling healthy behaviors from the top-down is also important. When managers feel supported on and off the job, they pass that on to team members.

Rethinking What Makes a Successful Manager

Finally, organizations need to redefine what success looks like for 21st century managers. Rather than promoting based on specific business outcomes, evaluate them based on leadership capabilities displayed, team member engagement, and diversity and inclusion gains. Provide ways for managers to give upward feedback to help senior leaders become more supportive.

Most importantly, destigmatize stepping down from management if it turns out not to be the right fit. Letting managers voluntarily go back to individual contributor roles shows it's a position requiring unique skills, not a higher status role. This empowers the right managers to step up while letting others return to non-managerial paths.

Conclusion

Reimagining the managerial pipeline requires comprehensive, long-term change management. However, the payoffs make it worthwhile. Organizations that implement rigorous, opt-in selection processes, robust development programs, and supportive systems will be rewarded with more engaged, higher-performing managers. In turn, their managers will be better equipped to lead teams to success amidst constant change.

While managers face challenges today, they are not insurmountable. By rethinking how we hire, train, and support the next generation of managers, organizations can ensure they have what it takes to lead in the 21st century. Managerial success is critical to organizational success. The time for reimagining the managerial pipeline is now.

Chapter 44

The Importance of Communicating Organizational Change

Organizational change is inevitable in today's fast-paced business environment. Mergers, acquisitions, restructurings, new technologies, and shifts in business strategies all require companies to frequently adapt and evolve. While change can be positive in driving innovation and growth, it can also create uncertainty and apprehension among employees if not handled properly. Surveys consistently show that many employees do not understand the reasons behind organizational changes, which can lead to resistance, decreased morale, and reduced productivity. Therefore, it is critical that leaders take the time to thoroughly explain upcoming changes and the rationale behind them.

In this chapter, we will explore how to effectively communicate important organizational changes to employees.

Inspire with a Compelling Vision

The first step in ushering in organizational change is to present a clear, inspiring vision of the future state. Leaders must paint a vivid picture of how the change will benefit the organization and employees. By tapping into emotions and values, an inspiring vision for the future can get employees excited about the possibilities ahead. For example, a healthcare company undergoing a digital transformation could explain how new technologies will help improve patient care and access. Appeals to making a positive societal impact can be powerful motivators. Leaders should tie the change to the organization's mission and identity. Employees want to feel like they are working towards something meaningful. Taking the time to craft and convey an inspiring vision sets the stage for employee buy-in down the road.

Provide Regular, Transparent Communication

After presenting the vision, leaders must follow through with frequent, open communication about the status of the change. Ongoing transparency helps build trust and prevent employees from filling information gaps with speculation and rumors. Communication should utilize multiple channels, including email updates, town halls, FAQs, and team meetings. Messages should come from multiple credible sources, like the CEO and direct managers. Some best practices for communication include:

- Share the reasons behind the change in detail. Explain how it will help the company succeed in the future.

- Be forthcoming about any potential downsides or challenges. Employees appreciate honesty.

- Provide a clear timeline laying out what will happen and when.

- Give regular progress updates on implementation activities.

- Be transparent about impacts on things like roles, responsibilities, structures, or workflows.

- Actively listen and respond to employee questions and concerns.

For example, during a system implementation, the project manager could provide weekly email updates on technical issues, user training schedules, and rollout dates. Frequent, tailored communication demonstrates the change is organized and thoughtful.

Empower Leaders to Lead Change

The message about organizational change must be reinforced by leaders at every level. Senior executives can introduce the vision, but direct managers serve a critical role in ensuring employee adoption. They must be empowered to lead their teams through change. This requires formal training and coaching for supervisors on communicating with empathy and leading in uncertain times. Managers should be equipped with detailed information on the change, talking points for their team, and guidance on addressing concerns. They must be available and approachable. Leaders should check in frequently with employees one-on-one to gauge reactions, clarify information, provide support, and highlight successes. A retail store undergoing new performance metrics would empower store managers by arming them with talking points, FAQs, training on giving feedback, and resources to recognize employee achievements. Empowered leaders can make change feel less imposed on employees.

Involve Employees Creatively

Finally, organizations should look for opportunities to engage employees directly in the change process. Involvement breeds commitment and makes the path forward feel less prescribed. There are many creative ways to solicit employee input and ideas when shaping a change initiative. Leaders can survey staff on what is working well versus what needs improvement, gather input on implementation options, or form employee advisory groups. During a new software rollout, an IT team could engage user groups to help design workflow changes, training programs, and rollout timelines. This not only improves solutions but builds inclusivity. Additionally, employees appreciate small involvement opportunities like volunteering for transition teams, pilot testing groups, or feedback forums. The more that employees feel heard and included in change, the more they will take ownership over its success.

Conclusion

Implementing organizational change initiatives successfully requires establishing a vision, communicating transparently, empowering leaders, and involving employees when possible. Leaders who take the time to thoroughly explain the reasoning and process behind change can gain critical employee buy-in and adoption. While change always brings some uncertainty and apprehension, following these best practices will help employees feel informed, supported, included, and inspired to contribute to a positive way forward. With persistence and care, leaders can guide their people through transitions while positioning the organization for future success.

355

Chapter 45

Overcoming the Solution Fixation Trap: Why Teams Need to Understand Problems Before Solving Them

As organizations face increasingly complex challenges, they are relying more and more on teams to tackle knotty issues and drive key decisions. To get the most value from team dynamics, leaders must be aware of biases that can undermine group decision-making, and take steps to actively guide teams through a sound process. One such bias is the "solution fixation trap," where teams jump into proposing solutions before fully grasping the problem. This trap can limit a team's perspective and lead to poor decisions. Teams are prone to spend too little time understanding problems before plunging into solutions. This leads them to focus on limited options and make choices that don't fully address the situation. To short-circuit this, leaders should take concrete steps to slow teams down, force deeper inquiry into problems, expand thinking, and only then let teams loose on solutions.

In this chapter, we will explore what the solution fixation trap looks like and how leaders can help teams avoid it.

The Solution Fixation Trap: Definition and Causes

In a recent study, researchers asked teams to solve a complex problem: improve the experience for families visiting an art museum. Some groups were given background on the problem, while others were given background plus suggested solutions. What they found was striking: teams that had received solutions spent less than half as much time (4 minutes versus 9 minutes) trying to understand the problem before jumping to solutions. They also proposed fewer unique solutions.

This demonstrated the solution fixation trap: when presented with potential answers, teams are biased toward those options. They spend less time inquiring into the problem, and their thinking narrows around the solutions presented rather than exploring the issue holistically.

The researchers attribute this to two cognitive shortcuts teams rely on to make complex decisions manageable: (1) Confirmation bias, where teams focus on information supporting the solutions at hand rather than challenging their assumptions, and (2) Availability bias, where readily available solutions strongly influence thinking. Together, these make it very hard for teams to deeply analyze the problem when potential solutions are already on the table.

The Risks of the Solution Fixation Trap

Succumbing to this trap carries significant risks. First, teams can pursue solutions not tailored to the problem, resulting in wasted time and money. Second, they may never understand the problem deeply enough to solve it effectively. Third, teams miss the chance to harness diverse perspectives, as their thinking converges narrowly on predetermined options. Finally, the group is more likely to default to the status quo rather than consider truly innovative directions.

For consequential organizational decisions, it's critical teams take the time to fully analyze the problem before settling on solutions. This expands thinking, surfaces key issues, and prevents teams from becoming anchored on limited options or assumptions. Only with a clear-eyed view of the problem can teams bring their full cognitive power to develop creative solutions tailored to the situation.

How Leaders Can Guide Teams Beyond the Trap

Leaders play a crucial role in helping teams avoid solution fixation. First, they must slow the team's rush to solutions. The authors suggest asking "Why do we need to solve this problem?" to spark deeper discussion. Leaders should also press teams to consider if they have framed the problem too narrowly or made unexamined assumptions. This expands perspectives and ensures the team fully leverages its diverse knowledge.

Second, leaders need to actively broaden thinking around solutions. If some options are already on the table, they should force teams to propose alternatives, even bad or counterintuitive ones. This breaks overreliance on the initial solutions. Leaders should also highlight how initial ideas fail to address key issues, pushing teams to reexamine them.

Finally, leaders must create space for teams to synthesize insights before solution-finding. After an expansive problem analysis, teams should be given time to identify key patterns and insights. This helps integrate diverse views into a shared understanding of the problem's core issues before turning to solutions. Jumping into solutions too quickly undermines this synthesis.

An example brings the risks of solution fixation to life. Consider a team that is tasked with increasing foot traffic to a retail clothing store. They are provided with two pre-defined options: run more television ads or offer deep discounts. The team jumps right into debating these solutions without digging into root causes of declining foot traffic, like increased local competition, a dated product lineup, or changing consumer habits. They end up pursuing ineffective TV ads and deep discounts that drive little traffic while failing to address the larger issues.

By contrast, with guidance from their leader, the team might instead have spent time analyzing the drop in foot traffic and its multiple complex drivers. This would have surfaced the need for product revamping, better local marketing, and an enhanced digital presence. Only then could they have developed an integrated solution tailored to the true problem.

Conclusion

In an increasingly complex business environment, leaders must maximize the value of teams by steering them away from cognitive traps like solution fixation. Left unguided, teams will gravitate toward obvious solutions rather than fully analyzing the problem. This leads to narrow, inferior decisions. Leaders can improve outcomes by slowing teams down, forcing deeper inquiry, expanding mindsets, and synthesizing insights before solution-finding. With problems thoroughly understood, teams can then bring their full creative power to develop tailored, innovative solutions and drive optimal organizational decisions. The solution fixation trap is a natural human tendency leaders must counteract, as a team that grasps the problem is better positioned to fix it.

363

Part 6

The Performance Journey

Chapter 46

Vision From Theory to Reality: Implementing the High-Performance Playbook

As we near the close of our journey unpacking strategies, models and inspirations for developing truly excellent organizations, it's only natural to feel both satisfied in new insights yet hungry for more. Like any role worth pursuing, the work of continuous progress demands perpetual learning and application far beyond the bounds of a single book. Yet I hope the frameworks, examples and discussions shared over preceding chapters have left you energized by the immense untapped potential within your teams.

The true test lies ahead in forming that vision into tangible ingrained habits fueling each person's daily efforts. In this concluding chapter, we'll synthesize key learnings around stewarding the implementation process to maximize long-term impact. My aim is to provide a roadmap for turning strategies into an autonomous, self-sustaining practice that outlives any single initiative. So let's begin charting the course towards fully realizing the performance playbook.

From the Top: Stewarding Commitment and Alignment

Research consistently shows top leadership support as the number one driver of success for any organizational change. As such, garnering executive buy-in and role-modeling principles represents a critical early step.

Schedule time for in-depth conversations to align on priorities, address reservations and secure budget/resource commitments. Co-create core messaging around why progression matters, focusing on higher purpose versus directives. Visibly demonstrate principles through actions like engaging diverse perspectives in strategic planning. These steps embed initiatives at the highest levels for long-term stewardship.

Empowered Execution Teams: Ownership Through Partnership

Appoint cross-functional, representative teams owning rollout within distinct business units or regions. Mix management and individual contributor roles to foster insight diversity.

Clearly define responsibilities centered on collaborating versus compliance, including establishing ongoing feedback channels. Equip teams with autonomy over customizing approaches while holding accountability for milestones. Regular coaching reinforces enabling environments where members autonomously drive progress.

Communication, Not Mandates: Inspiring Intrinsic Motivation

Research shows directives produce short-term impacts but intrinsic drive achieves permanence. Embed progress narratives within day-to-day conversations versus separate programming.

Profile exemplars living principles through localized campaigns highlighting impacts. Launch interactive forums applying learnings to real issues sparking empowerment. Recognize supporters' integral roles versus external factors for success. Inspire viewing difficulties as opportunities inherent to growth versus setbacks.

Measuring What Matters: Continuous Improvement Cycles

Rather than endpoints, define implementation as an ongoing systems evolution. Co-design qualitative and quantitative metrics valuing capabilities like agility versus outputs alone.

Debrief quarterly utilizing feedback to iteratively sharpen approaches through small prototypes. Automate and gamify progress tracking for transparency and fun. Annual reviews correlate efforts to strategy execution and talent outcomes revealing areas demanding recalibration over time.

Progress Realized: A Continuous Habit

In closing, sustainable excellence stems not from any singular event but rather cultivating an intrinsic ideology where people autonomously chart both individual advancement and collective audacity. The insights shared here offer but one vantage - you hold the profound responsibility of shaping their ultimate impact within your unique environments and relationships.

Always remember strategy implementation as less a checklist and more an emergent practice continually redefined through partnership. With commitment to that dynamic spirit, I'm confident your teams can realize heights yet unimagined. Now go forth and actualize and refine that limitless potential and progress in your daily pursuits. The journey of continual growth has only just begun.

ABOUT THE AUTHOR

Jonathan H. Westover, Ph.D. is a 16X best-selling and award-winning author and podcaster, ranked # 1 HR, Innovation, and Future of Work industry thought leader (Thinkers360), ranked in the Top 30 in Management and Organizational Culture (Global Gurus), and ranked in the top 20 of global researchers in the following topic areas - "Future of Work," "Global Leadership," "Organizational Development, "Public Service Motivation," and "Social Impact" (Google Scholar). Additionally, ScholarGPS has ranked him the #18 scholar in the world for job satisfaction research. LeadersHum put him on their Power List of the Top 200 Biggest Voices in Leadership to watch. He is an entrepreneur, management consultant, teacher, and research academic based in Orem, Utah. He serves on a host of nonprofit, community, and association boards and committees and has received numerous awards for his teaching, research, and service to the community.

Current Professional Roles

Academic: Dr. Westover is a professor and chair of Organizational Leadership in the Woodbury School of Business at Utah Valley University, Academic Director of the UVU Center for Social Impact and the UVU SIMLab, Director of

Academic Service-Learning in the UVU Innovation Academy, and a Faculty Industry Impact Fellow in the Women in Business Impact Lab. He is Vice President and member of the Executive Committee of the Western Academy of Management, and he is an affiliate faculty member in UVU's Integrated Students, Master of Public Administration, and Master of Business Administration programs. Dr. Westover has been published widely in academic journals, books, and practitioner publications. He is a regular visiting faculty member in other international graduate business programs.

Consulting: Jonathan is an experienced organizational leadership, people management, and organizational development consultant and managing partner and principal at Human Capital Innovations. For two decades, he has worked to help transform organizations across the globe. He is also the producer and host of the Human Capital Leadership (HCI) Podcast and Managing Editor of the Human Capital Leadership Magazine. Previously, Jonathan was an external consultant with the firm Targeted Learning, and an internal consultant in the Human Resource Development office at Brigham Young University, in the corporate Organizational Development office at InterContinental Hotels, and in the corporate Organizational Development office at LG Electronics in Gumi, South Korea.

Thought Leadership: Jonathan is a member of the Forbes Coaches Council, a member of the Harvard Business Review Advisory Council, Non-Resident Fellow in Social and Development Policy with the Nkafu Policy Institute (part of the Denis & Lenora Foretia Foundation), member of the HR Certification Institute CEO Advisory Council and past member of the board of directors, member of the Humantelligence Scientific Advisory, Board Chair and Director of the Corporate Division of the Global Listening Centre, a CIPD Academic Fellow, and an Advance HE Senior Fellow. Jonathan has been published widely and quoted as a management expert in popular and professional media locally, nationally, and abroad (such as Forbes, The Economist, U.S. News and World Report, The Wall Street Journal, MSNBC, PBS, NBC, CBS, ABC, FOX, MarketWatch, HR.com, SHRM.org, HRCI.org, The Washington Post, and USA Today).

Education

Jonathan received his Bachelor of Science degree in Sociology - Research and Analysis (with minors in management and Korean) from the College of Family, Home, and Social Sciences and his Master of Public Administration degree (emphases in Organizational Behavior and Human Resource Management) from the Marriott School of Management at Brigham Young University. He received his Ph.D. in Sociology (emphases in International Political Economy and Work and Organizations) from the College of Social and Behavioral Science at the University of Utah. He has also received graduate certificates in demography and higher education teaching from the University of Utah.